LETTERS

OF

EMILY DICKINSON

EDITED BY

MABEL LOOMIS TODD

IN TWO VOLUMES

VOLUME I

BOSTON

ROBERTS BROTHERS

1894

University Press
John Wilson and Son, Cambridge, U.S.A.

TABLE OF CONTENTS

VOLUME I

———◆———

LIST OF ILLUSTRATIONS

————◆————

INTRODUCTORY

THE lovers of Emily Dickinson's poems have been so eager for her prose that her sister has gathered these letters, and committed their preparation to me.

Emily Dickinson's verses, often but the reflection of a passing mood, do not always completely represent herself, — rarely, indeed, showing the dainty humor, the frolicsome gayety, which continually bubbled over in her daily life. The sombre and even weird outlook upon this world and the next, characteristic of many of the poems, was by no means a prevailing condition of mind; for, while fully apprehending all the tragic elements in life, enthusiasm and bright joyousness were yet her normal qualities, and stimulating moral heights her native dwelling-place. All this may be glimpsed in her letters, no less full of charm, it is believed, to the general reader, than to Emily Dickinson's personal friends. As she kept no journal, the letters are the more interesting because they contain all the prose which she is known to have written.

It was with something almost like dread that I approached the task of arranging these letters, lest the deep revelations of a peculiarly shy inner life might so pervade them that in true loyalty to their writer none could be publicly used. But with few exceptions they have been read and prepared with entire relief from that feeling, and with unshrinking pleasure ; the sanctities were not invaded. Emily kept her little reserves, and bared her soul but seldom, even in intimate correspondence. It was not so much that she was always on spiritual guard, as that she sported with her varying moods, and tested them upon her friends with apparent delight in the effect, as airy and playful as it was half unconscious.

So large is the number of letters to each of several correspondents, that it has seemed best to place these sets in separate chapters. The continuity is perhaps more perfectly preserved in this way than by the usual method of mere chronological succession ; especially as, in a life singularly uneventful, no marked periods of travel or achievement serve otherwise to classify them. On this plan a certain order has been possible, too ; the opening letters in each chapter are always later than the first of the preceding, although the last letters of one reach a date beyond the beginning of the next. The less remarkable writing, of course, fills the first chapters ; but even this shows her love of study, of Nature, and a devotion to home almost as intense as in strange Emily Brontë.

Nothing is perhaps more marked than the change of style between the diffuseness of girlhood and the brilliant sententiousness of late middle life, often startlingly unexpected. And yet suggestions of future picturesque and epigrammatic power occasionally flash through the long, youthful correspondence. Lowell once wrote of the first letters of Carlyle, 'The man . . . is all there in the earliest of his writing that we have (potentially there, in character wholly there).' It is chiefly for these 'potential' promises that Emily Dickinson's girlish letters are included, all the variations in the evolution of a style having hardly less interest for the student of human nature than of literature. Village life, even in a college town, was very democratic in the early days when the first of these letters were written, and they suggest a refreshing atmosphere of homely simplicity.

Unusual difficulties have been encountered in arranging the letters with definite reference to years, as none but the very earliest were dated. The change in handwriting, of which specimens are given in facsimile, was no less noticeable than Emily Dickinson's development in literary style ; and this alone has been a general guide. The thoughtfulness of a few correspondents in recording the time of the letters' reception has been a farther and most welcome assistance ; while occasionally the kind of postage-stamp and the postmark helped to indicate when they were written, although generally the enve-

lopes had not been preserved. But the larger part
have been placed by searching out the dates of
contemporaneous incidents mentioned, — for instance, numerous births, marriages, and deaths;
any epoch in the life of a friend was an event to
Emily Dickinson, always noticed by a bit of flashing
verse, or a graceful, if mystically expressed, note of
comfort or congratulation. If errors are found in
assignment to the proper time, it will not be from
lack of having interrogated all available sources of
information.

In more recent years, dashes instead of punctuation, and capitals for all important words, together
with the quaint handwriting, give to the actual
manuscript an individual fascination quite irresistible. But the coldness of print destroys that
elusive charm, so that dashes and capitals have been
restored to their conventional use.

In her later years, Emily Dickinson rarely addressed the envelopes : it seemed as if her sensitive
nature shrank from the publicity which even her
handwriting would undergo, in the observation of
indifferent eyes. Various expedients were resorted
to, — obliging friends frequently performed this office
for her; sometimes a printed newspaper label was
pasted upon the envelope ; but the actual strokes
of her own pencil were, so far as possible, reserved
exclusively for friendly eyes.

Emily Dickinson's great disinclination for an exposition of the theology current during her girlhood

is matter for small wonder. While her fathers were men of recognized originality and force, they did not question the religious teaching of the time; they were leaders in town and church, even strict and uncompromising in their piety. Reverence for accepted ways and forms, merely as such, seems entirely to have been left out of Emily's constitution. To her, God was not a far-away and dreary Power to be daily addressed, — the great 'Eclipse' of which she wrote, — but He was near and familiar and pervasive. Her garden was full of His brightness and glory; the birds sang and the sky glowed because of Him. To shut herself out of the sunshine in a church, dark, chilly, restricted, was rather to shut herself away from Him; almost pathetically she wrote, 'I believe the love of God may be taught not to seem like bears.'

In essence, no real irreverence mars her poems or her letters. Of malice aforethought, — an intentional irreverence, — she is never once guilty. The old interpretation of the biblical estimate of life was cause to her for gentle, wide-eyed astonishment. No one knew better the phrases which had become cant, and which seemed always to misrepresent the Father Whom she knew with personal directness and without necessity for human intervention. It was a theologically misconceived idea of a 'jealous God,' for which she had a profound contempt; and the fact that those ideas were still held by the stricter New England people of her day made not the

slightest difference in her expression of disapproval.
Fearless and daring, she had biblical quotation at
her finger-tips ; and even if she sometimes used it
in a way which might shock a conventionalist, she
had in her heart too profound an adoration for the
great, ever-living, and present Father to hold a
shadow of real irreverence toward Him, so peculiarly near.   No soul in which dwelt not a very
noble and actual love and respect for the essen-
tials could have written as she did of real triumph,
of truth, of aspiration.

> 'We never know how high we are,
>   Till we are called to rise ;
> And then, if we are true to plan,
>   Our statures touch the skies.
>
> 'The heroism we recite
>   Would be a daily thing
> Did not ourselves the cubits warp,
>   For fear to be a king.'

Must not one who wrote that have had her ever-
open shrine, her reverenced tribunal ?

The whims and pretences of society, its forms
and unrealities, seemed to her thin and unworthy.
Conventionalities, while they amused, exasperated
her also ; and the little poem beginning,

> 'The show is not the show,
>   But they that go,'

expresses in large measure her attitude toward society, when she lived in the midst of it.   Real life,
on the other hand, seemed vast and inexpressibly

solemn. Petty trivialities had no part in her constitution, and she came to despise them more and more, — so much, indeed, that with her increasing shyness, she gradually gave up all journeys, and finally retired completely from even the simple life of a New England college town.

As has been said of Emily Brontë, ' To this natural isolation of spirit we are in a great measure indebted for that passionate love of Nature which gives such a vivid reality and exquisite simplicity to her descriptions.' Emily Dickinson's letters, almost as much as the poems, exhibit her elf-like intimacy with Nature. She sees and apprehends the great mother's processes, and shares the rapture of all created things under the wide sky. The letters speak of flowers, of pines and autumnal colors ; but no natural sight or sound or incident seems to have escaped her delicate apprehension.

Bird songs, crickets, frost, and winter winds, even the toad and snake, mushrooms and bats, have an indescribable charm for her, which she in turn brings to us. March, 'that month of proclamation,' was especially dear ; and among her still unpublished verses is a characteristic greeting to the windy month. In all its aspects ' Nature became the unique charm and consolation of her life, and as such she has written of it.'

Warm thanks are due the friends who have generously lent letters for reproduction. That they were friends of Emily Dickinson, and willing to

share her words with the larger outside circle, waiting and appreciative, entitles them to the gratitude,
not merely of the Editor, but of all who make up
the world that Emily 'never saw,' but to which,
nevertheless, she sent a 'message.'

MABEL LOOMIS TODD

AMHERST, MASSACHUSETTS
October 1894

LETTERS OF EMILY DICKINSON

———◆———

CHAPTER I

To Mrs A. P. Strong

THE letters in this chapter were written to a schoolmate and early friend. The first is one of the oldest yet found, dated when Emily Dickinson had but recently passed her fourteenth birthday.

Before the era of outer envelopes, it is quaintly written on a large square sheet, and so folded that the fourth page forms a cover bearing the address. Most of the remaining letters to Mrs Strong are thus folded, and sealed either with wax or wafers, — occasionally with little rectangular or diamond papers bearing mottoes stamped in gold. The handwriting is almost microscopic, the pages entirely filled. Merely personal items have been generally omitted.

It will be seen that the name 'Emilie E. Dickinson' is sometimes used. The *ie* was a youthful vagary, and the second initial, E., stood for Elizabeth, a 'middle name' entirely discarded in later years.

AMHERST, Feb. 23, 1845.

DEAR A., — After receiving the smitings of conscience for a long time, I have at length succeeded in stifling the voice of that faithful monitor by a promise of a long letter to you; so leave everything and sit down prepared for a long siege in the shape of a bundle of nonsense from friend E.

. . . I keep your lock of hair as precious as gold and a great deal more so. I often look at it when I go to my little lot of treasures, and wish the owner of that glossy lock were here. Old Time wags on pretty much as usual at Amherst, and I know of nothing that has occurred to break the silence; however, the reduction of the postage has excited my risibles somewhat. Only think! We can send a letter before long for five little coppers only, filled with the thoughts and advice of dear friends. But I will not get into a philosophizing strain just yet. There is time enough for that upon another page of this mammoth sheet. . . . Your *beau idéal* D. I have not seen lately. I presume he was changed into a star some night while gazing at them, and placed in the constellation Orion between Bellatrix and Betelgeux. I doubt not if he was here he would wish to be kindly remembered to you. What delightful weather we have had for a week!

It seems more like smiling May crowned with flowers than cold, arctic February wading through snow-
drifts. I have heard some sweet little birds sing,
but I fear we shall have more cold weather and their
little bills will be frozen up before their songs are
finished. My plants look beautifully. Old King
Frost has not had the pleasure of snatching any of
them in his cold embrace as yet, and I hope will
not. Our little pussy has made out to live. I believe
you know what a fatality attends our little kitties, all
of them, having had six die one right after the other.
Do you love your little niece J. as well as ever?
Your soliloquy on the year that is past and gone was
not unheeded by me. Would that we might spend
the year which is now fleeting so swiftly by to better
advantage than the one which we have not the power
to recall! Now I know you will laugh, and say I
wonder what makes Emily so sentimental. But I
don't care if you do, for I sha'n't hear you. What
are you doing this winter? I am about everything.
I am now working a pair of slippers to adorn my
father's feet. I wish you would come and help me
finish them. . . . Although it is late in the day, I
am going to wish you a happy New Year, — not but
what I think your New Year will pass just as happily
without it, but to make a little return for your kind
wish, which so far in a good many respects has been
granted, probably because you wished that it might
be so. . . . I go to singing-school Sabbath evenings
to improve my voice. Don't you envy me? . . .

I wish you would come and make me a long visit. If you will, I will entertain you to the best of my abilities, which you know are neither few nor small. Why can't you persuade your father and mother to let you come here to school next term, and keep me company, as I am going? Miss ——, I presume you can guess who I mean, is going to finish her education next summer. The finishing stroke is to be put on at Newton. She will then have learned all that we poor foot-travellers are toiling up the hill of knowledge to acquire. Wonderful thought! Her horse has carried her along so swiftly that she has nearly gained the summit, and we are plodding along on foot after her. Well said and sufficient this. We 'll finish an education sometime, won't we? You may then be Plato, and I will be Socrates, provided you won't be wiser than I am. Lavinia just now interrupted my flow of thought by saying give my love to A. I presume you will be glad to have some one break off this epistle. All the girls send much love to you. And please accept a large share for yourself.   From your beloved

EMILY E. DICKINSON.

Please send me a copy of that Romance you were writing at Amherst. I am in a fever to read it. I expect it will be against my Whig feelings.

After this postscript many others follow, across the top, down the edges, tucked in

wherever space will allow. There are also a
few lines from each of three girl friends to
'dear A.'

AMHERST, May 7, 1845.

DEAR A., — It seems almost an age since I have
seen you, and it is indeed an age for friends to be
separated.   I was delighted to receive a paper from
you, and I also was much pleased with the news it
contained, especially that you are taking lessons on
the 'piny,' as you always call it. But remember not to
get on ahead of me. Father intends to have a piano
very soon. How happy I shall be when I have one
of my own ! Old Father Time has wrought many
changes here since your last short visit. Miss S. T.
and Miss N. M. have both taken the marriage vows
upon themselves. Dr Hitchcock has moved into
his new house, and Mr Tyler across the way from
our house has moved into President Hitchcock's old
house. Mr C. is going to move into Mr T.'s former
house, but the worst thing old Time has done here is
he has walked so fast as to overtake H. M. and carry
her to Hartford on last week Saturday. I was so
vexed with him for it that I ran after him and made
out to get near enough to him to put some salt on
his tail, when he fled and left me to run home alone.
. . . Viny went to Boston this morning with father,
to be gone a fortnight, and I am left alone in all my
glory. I suppose she has got there before this time,
and is probably staring with mouth and eyes wide

open at the wonders of the city. I have been to walk to-night, and got some very choice wild flowers. I wish you had some of them. Viny and I both go to school this term. We have a very fine school. There are 63 scholars. I have four studies. They are Mental Philosophy, Geology, Latin, and Botany. How large they sound, don't they? I don't believe you have such big studies. . . . My plants look finely now. I am going to send you a little geranium leaf in this letter, which you must press for me. Have you made you an herbarium yet? I hope you will if you have not, it would be such a treasure to you; 'most all the girls are making one. If you do, perhaps I can make some additions to it from flowers growing around here. How do you enjoy your school this term? Are the teachers as pleasant as our old school-teachers? I expect you have a great many prim, starched up young ladies there, who, I doubt not, are perfect models of propriety and good behavior. If they are, don't let your free spirit be chained by them. I don't know as there [are] any in school of this stamp. But there 'most always are a few, whom the teachers look up to and regard as their satellites. I am growing handsome very fast indeed! I expect I shall be the belle of Amherst when I reach my 17th year. I don't doubt that I shall have perfect crowds of admirers at that age. Then how I shall delight to make them await my bidding, and with what delight shall I witness their suspense while I make my final decision. But away with my non-

sense. I have written one composition this term,
and I need not assure you it was exceedingly edify-
ing to myself as well as everybody else. Don't you
want to see it? I really wish you could have a
chance. We are obliged to write compositions once
in a fortnight, and select a piece to read from
some interesting book the week that we don't write
compositions.

We really have some most charming young women
in school this term. I sha'n't call them anything
but women, for women they are in every sense of
the word. I must, however, describe one, and while
I describe her I wish Imagination, who is ever present with you, to make a little picture of this self-same
young lady in your mind, and by her aid see if you
cannot conceive how she looks. Well, to begin. . . .
Then just imagine her as she is, and a huge string of
gold beads encircling her neck, and don't she present
a lively picture ; and then she is so bustling, she is
always whizzing about, and whenever I come in con-
tact with her I really think I am in a hornet's nest.
I can't help thinking every time I see this singular
piece of humanity of Shakespeare's description of a
tempest in a teapot. But I must not laugh about
her, for I verily believe she has a good heart, and
that is the principal thing now-a-days. Don't you
hope I shall become wiser in the company of such
virtuosos? It would certainly be desirable. Have
you noticed how beautifully the trees look now?
They seem to be completely covered with fragrant

blossoms. . . . I had so many things to do for Viny, as she was going away, that very much against my wishes I deferred writing you until now, but forgive and forget, dear A., and I will promise to do better in future. Do write me soon, and let it be a long, long letter; and when you can't get time to write, send a paper, so as to let me know you think of me still, though we are separated by hill and stream. All the girls send much love to you. Don't forget to let me receive a letter from you soon. I can say no more now as my paper is all filled up.

Your affectionate friend,

EMILY E. DICKINSON.

[Written in 1845; postmarked Amherst, August 4.]

Sabbath Eve.

DEAR A., — I have now sat down to write you a long, long letter. My writing apparatus is upon a stand before me, and all things are ready. I have no flowers before me as you had to inspire you. But then you know I can imagine myself inspired by them, and perhaps that will do as well. You cannot imagine how delighted I was to receive your letter. It was so full, and everything in it was interesting to me because it came from you. I presume you did not doubt my gratitude for it, on account of my delaying so long to answer it, for you know I have had no leisure for anything. When I tell you that our term has been eleven weeks long, and that I have had four studies and taken music lessons, you

can imagine a little how my time has been taken up
lately. I will try to be more punctual in such matters for the future. How are you now? I am very
sorry to hear that you are unable to remain in your
school on account of your health, it must be such
a disappointment to you. But I presume you are
enjoying yourself much to be at home again. You
asked me in your last letter if old Father Time
wagged on in Amherst pretty much as ever. For
my part, I see no particular change in his move-
ments unless it be that he goes on a swifter pace
than formerly, and that he wields his sickle more
sternly than ever. How do you like taking music
lessons? I presume you are delighted with it. I
am taking lessons this term of Aunt S——, who is
spending the summer with us. I never enjoyed
myself more than I have this summer; for we
have had such a delightful school and such pleasant
teachers, and besides I have had a piano of my
own. Our examination is to come off next week
on Monday. I wish you could be here at that time.
Why can't you come? If you will, you can come
and practise on my piano as much as you wish to.
I am already gasping in view of our examination;
and although I am determined not to dread it I
know it is so foolish, yet in spite of my heroic resolutions, I cannot avoid a few misgivings when I
think of those tall, stern trustees, and when I know
that I shall lose my character if I don't recite as
precisely as the laws of the Medes and Persians.

But what matter will that be a hundred years hence? I will distress you no longer with my fears, for you know well enough what they are without my entering into any explanations. Are you practising now you are at home? I hope you are, for if you are not you would be likely to forget what you have learnt. I want very much to hear you play. I have the same instruction book that you have, Bertini, and I am getting along in it very well. Aunt S—— says she sha'n't let me have many tunes now, for she wants I should get over in the book a good ways first. Oh, A., if Sarah G——, H——, and yourself were only here this summer, what times we should have! I wish if we can't be together all the time that we could meet once in a while at least. I wish you would all come to our house, and such times as we would have would be a caution. I want to see you all so much that it seems as if I could not wait. Have you heard anything from Miss Adams, our dear teacher? How much I would give to see her once more, but I am afraid I never shall. She is so far away. You asked me in your letter to tell you all the news worth telling, and although there is not much, yet I will endeavor to think of everything that will be new to you. In the first place, Mrs J. and Mrs S. M. have both of them a little daughter. Very promising children, I understand. I don't doubt if they live they will be ornaments to society. I think they are both to be considered as embryos of future usefulness. Mrs W. M. has

now two grand-daughters. Is n't she to be envied?
. . . I am sorry that you are laying up H.'s sins
against her. I think you had better heap coals of
fire upon her head by writing to her constantly until
you get an answer. I have some patience with
these 'school marms.' They have so many trials.
I hope you will decide to blot out her iniquities
against her. I don't know about this Mr E. giving you concert tickets. I think for my part it
looks rather suspicious. He is a young man, I suppose. These music teachers are always such high-
souled beings that I think they would exactly suit
your fancy. My garden looks beautifully now. I
wish you could see it. I would send you a bouquet
if I could get a good opportunity. My house plants
look very finely, too. You wished me to give you
some account of S. P. She is attending school this
term and studying Latin and Algebra. She is very
well and happy and sends much love to you. All
the girls send much love to you, and wish you to
write to them. I have been working a beautiful
book-mark to give to one of our school-girls. Perhaps you have seen it. It is an arrow with a beautiful wreath around it. Have you altered any since
I have seen you? Is n't it a funny question for one
friend to ask another? I have n't altered any, I
think, except that I have my hair done up, and that
makes me look different. I can imagine just how
you look now. I wonder what you are doing this
moment. I have got an idea that you are knitting

edging. Are you? Won't you tell me when you answer my letter whether I guessed right or not? . . . You gave me a compliment in your letter in regard to my being a faithful correspondent. I must say I think I deserve it. I have been learning several beautiful pieces lately. The 'Grave of Bonaparte' is one, 'Lancers Quickstep,' and 'Maiden, weep no more,' which is a sweet little song. I wish much to see you and hear you play. I hope you will come to A. before long. Why can't you pass commencement here? I do wish you would. . . . I have looked my letter over, and find I have written nothing worth reading. . . . Accept much love from your affectionate friend,

                                        EMILY E. D.

Thursday, Sept. 26, 1845.

DEAREST A., — As I just glanced at the clock and saw how smoothly the little hands glide over the surface, I could scarcely believe that those self-same little hands had eloped with so many of my precious moments since I received your affectionate letter, and it was still harder for me to believe that I, who am always boasting of being so faithful a correspondent, should have been guilty of negligence in so long delaying to answer it. . . . I am very glad to hear that you are better than you have been, and I hope in future disease will not be as neighborly as he has been heretofore to either of us. I long to see you, dear A., and speak with you face

to face ; but so long as a bodily interview is denied
us, we must make letters answer, though it is hard
for friends to be separated. I really believe you
would have been frightened to have heard me scold.
when Sabra informed me that you had decided not
to visit Amherst this fall. But as I could find no
one upon whom to vent my spleen for your decision,
I thought it best to be calm, and therefore have at
length resigned myself to my cruel fate, though with
not a very good grace. I think' you do well to
inquire whether anything has been heard from H.
I really don't know what has become of her, unless
procrastination has carried her off. I think that
must be the case. I think you have given quite a
novel description of the wedding. Are you quite
sure Mr F., the minister, told them to stand up and
he would tie them in a great bow-knot? But I beg
pardon for speaking so lightly of so solemn a cere-
mony. You asked me in your letter if I did not
think you partial in your admiration of Miss Helen
H., ditto Mrs P. I answer, Not in the least. She
was universally beloved in Amherst. She made us
quite a visit in June, and we regretted more than
ever that she was going where we could not see her
as often as we had been accustomed. She seemed
very happy in her prospects, and seemed to think
distance nothing in comparison to a home with the
one of her choice. I hope she will be happy,
and of course she will. I wished much to see her
once more, but was denied the privilege. . . . You

asked me if I was attending school now. I am not. Mother thinks me not able to confine myself to school this term. She had rather I would exercise, and I can assure you I get plenty of that article by staying at home. I am going to learn to make bread to-morrow. So you may imagine me with my sleeves rolled up, mixing flour, milk, saleratus, etc., with a deal of grace. I advise you if you don't know how to make the staff of life to learn with dispatch. I think I could keep house very comfortably if I knew how to cook. But as long as I don't, my knowledge of housekeeping is about of as much use as faith without works, which you know we are told is dead. Excuse my quoting from Scripture, dear A., for it was so handy in this case I could n't get along very well without it. Since I wrote you last, the summer is past and gone, and autumn with the sere and yellow leaf is already upon us. I never knew the time to pass so swiftly, it seems to me, as the past summer. I really think some one must have oiled his chariot wheels, for I don't recollect of hearing him pass, and I am sure I should if something had not prevented his chariot wheels from creaking as usual. But I will not expatiate upon him any longer, for I know it is wicked to trifle with so revered a personage, and I fear he will make me a call in person to inquire as to the remarks which I have made concerning him. Therefore I will let him alone for the present. . . . How are you getting on with your music? Well, I hope and trust. I am taking lessons and am getting along very well, and now I have a piano, I am very happy. I feel much honored at having even a doll named for me. I believe I shall have to give it a silver cup, as that is the custom among old ladies when a child is named for them. . . . Have you any flowers now? I have had a beautiful flower-garden this summer; but they are nearly gone now. It is very cold to-night, and I mean to pick the prettiest ones before I go to bed, and cheat Jack Frost of so many of *the treasures* he calculates to rob to-night. Won't it be a capital idea to put him at defiance, for once at least, if no more? I would love to send you a bouquet if I had an opportunity, and you could press it and write under it, The last flowers of summer. Would n't it be poetical, and you know that is what young ladies aim to be now-a-days. . . . I expect I have altered a good deal since I have seen you, dear A. I have grown tall a good deal, and wear my golden tresses done up in a net-cap. Modesty, you know, forbids me to mention whether my personal appearance has altered. I leave that for others to judge. But my [word omitted] has not changed, nor will it in time to come. I shall always remain the same old six-pence. . . . I can say no more now, as it is after ten, and everybody has gone to bed but me. Don't forget your affectionate friend,

EMILY E. D.

AMHERST, Jan. 12, 1846.

A., MY DEAR, — Since I received your precious letter another year has commenced its course, and the old year has gone never to return. How sad it makes one feel to sit down quietly and think of the flight of the old year, and the unceremonious obtrusion of the new year upon our notice! How many things we have omitted to do which might have cheered a human heart, or whispered hope in the ear of the sorrowful, and how many things have we done over which the dark mantle of regret will ever fall! How many good resolutions did I make at the commencement of the year now flown, merely to break them and to feel more than ever convinced of the weakness of my own resolutions! The New Year's day was unusually gloomy to me, I know not why, and perhaps for that reason a host of unpleasant reflections forced themselves upon me which I found not easy to throw off. But I will no longer sentimentalize upon the past, for I cannot recall it. I will, after inquiring for the health of my dear A., relapse into a more lively strain. I can hardly have patience to write, for I have not seen you for so long that I have worlds of things to tell you, and my pen is not swift enough to answer my purpose at all. However, I will try to make it communicate as much information as possible and wait to see your own dear self once more before I relate all my thoughts which have come and gone since I last saw you. I suppose

from your letter that you are enjoying yourself finely
this winter at Miss C.'s school.   I would give a great
deal if I was there with you.   I don't go to school
this winter except to a recitation in German.   Mr
C. has a very large class, and father thought I might
never have another opportunity to study it.   It
takes about an hour and a half to recite.   Then I
take music lessons and practise two hours in a day,
and besides these two I have a large stand of plants
to cultivate.   This is the principal round of my
occupation this winter. . . . I have just seen a
funeral procession go by of a negro baby, so if my
ideas are rather dark you need not marvel. . . .
Old Santa Claus was very polite to me the last
Christmas.   I hung up my stocking on the bed-
post as usual.   I had a perfume bag and a bottle
of otto of rose to go with it, a sheet of music,
a china mug with *Forget me not* upon it, from
S. S., — who, by the way, is as handsome, enter-
taining, and as fine a piano player as in former
times, — a toilet cushion, a watch case, a fortune-
teller, and an amaranthine stock of pin-cushions and
needlebooks, which in ingenuity and art would rival
the works of Scripture Dorcas.   I found abundance
of candy in my stocking, which I do not think has
had the anticipated effect upon my disposition, in
case it was to sweeten it, also two hearts at the
bottom of all, which I thought looked rather omi-
nous; but I will not enter into any more details, for
they take up more room than I can spare.

Have n't we had delightful weather for a week or two? It seems as if Old Winter had forgotten himself. Don't you believe he is absent-minded? It has been bad weather for colds, however. I have had a severe cold for a few days, and can sympathize with you, though I have been delivered from a stiff neck. I think you must belong to the tribe of Israel, for you know in the Bible the prophet calls them a stiff-necked generation. I have lately come to the conclusion that I am Eve, alias Mrs Adam. You know there is no account of her death in the Bible, and why am not I Eve? If you find any statements which you think likely to prove the truth of the case, I wish you would send them to me without delay.

Have you heard a word from H. M. or S. T.? I consider them lost sheep. I send them a paper every week on Monday, but I never get one in return. I am almost a mind to take a hand-car and go around to hunt them up. I can't think that they have forgotten us, and I know of no reason unless they are sick why they should delay so long to show any signs of remembrance. Do write me soon a very long letter, and tell me all about your school and yourself too.

> Your affectionate friend,
> EMILY E. DICKINSON.

Friday Eve [summer], 1846.

MY DEAR A., — Though it is a long time since I received your affectionate epistle, yet when I give you my reasons for my long delay, I know you will freely forgive and forget all past offences.

It seems to me that time has never flown so swiftly with me as it has the last spring. I have been busy every minute, and not only so, but hurried all the time. So you may imagine that I have not had a spare moment, much though my heart has longed for it, to commune with an absent friend. . . . I presume you will be wondering by this time what I am doing to be in so much haste as I have declared myself to be. Well, I will tell you. I am fitting to go to South Hadley Seminary, and expect if my health is good to enter that institution a year from next fall. Are you not astonished to hear such news? You cannot imagine how much I am anticipating in entering there. It has been in my thought by day, and my dreams by night, ever since I heard of South Hadley Seminary. I fear I am anticipating too much, and that some freak of fortune may overturn all my airy schemes for future happiness. But it is my nature always to anticipate more than I realize. . . . Have you not heard that Miss Adams — dear Miss Adams — is here this term? Oh, you cannot imagine how natural it seems to see her happy face in school once more. But it needs Harriet, Sarah, and your own dear self to complete the ancient picture. I hope we shall get you all back before Miss Adams goes away again. Have you yet heard a word from that prodigal, — H. ? . . .

Your affectionate friend,

EMILY E. D.

I send you a memento in the form of a pressed flower, which you must keep.

A converted Jew has been lecturing here for the last week. His lectures were free, and they were on the present condition of the Jews. Dr Scudder, a returned missionary, is here now, and he is lecturing also. Have you seen a beautiful piece of poetry which has been going through the papers lately? *Are we almost there?* is the title of it. . . . I have two hours to practise daily now I am in school. I have been learning a beautiful thing, which I long to have you hear. . . .

BOSTON, Sept. 8, 1846.

MY DEAR FRIEND A., — It is a long, long time since I received your welcome letter, and it becomes me to sue for forgiveness, which I am sure your affectionate heart will not refuse to grant. But many and unforeseen circumstances have caused my long delay. . . . Father and mother thought a journey would be of service to me, and accordingly I left home for Boston week before last. I had a delightful ride in the cars, and am now getting settled down, if there can be such a state in the city. I am visiting in my aunt's family, and am happy. Happy! did I say? No; not happy, but contented. I have been here a fortnight to-day, and in that time I have both seen and heard a great many wonderful things. Perhaps you might like to know how I have spent the time here. I have

been to Mount Auburn, to the Chinese Museum, to
Bunker Hill; I have attended two concerts and one
Horticultural Exhibition.   I have been upon the
top of the State House, and almost everywhere that
you can imagine.   Have you ever been to Mount
Auburn?   If not, you can form but slight con-
ception of this ' City of the Dead.'   It seems as if
nature had formed this spot with a distinct idea in
view of its being a resting-place for her children,
where, wearied and disappointed, they might stretch
themselves beneath the spreading cypress, and close
their eyes ' calmly as to a night's repose, or flowers
at set of sun.'

The Chinese Museum is a great curiosity.   There
are an endless variety of wax figures made to re-
semble the Chinese, and dressed in their costume.
Also articles of Chinese manufacture of an innu-
merable variety deck the rooms.   Two of the
Chinese go with this exhibition.   One of them is a
professor of music in China, and the other is teacher
of a writing-school at home.   They were both
wealthy, and not obliged to labor, but they were
also opium-eaters ; and fearing to continue the practice lest it destroyed their lives, yet unable to
break the ' rigid chain of habit ' in their own land,
they left their families, and came to this country.
They have now entirely overcome the practice.
There is something peculiarly interesting to me in
their self-denial.   The musician played upon two of
his instruments, and accompanied them with his

voice. It needed great command over my risible faculties to enable me to keep sober as this amateur was performing ; yet he was so very polite to give us some of his native music that we could not do otherwise than to express ourselves highly edified with his performances. The writing-master is constantly occupied in writing the names of visitors who request it, upon cards in the Chinese language, for which he charges 12½ cents apiece. He never fails to give his card besides to the persons who wish it. I obtained one of his cards for Viny and myself, and I consider them very precious. Are you still in Norwich, and attending to music? I am not now taking lessons, but I expect to when I return home.

Does it seem as though September had come? How swiftly summer has fled, and what report has it borne to heaven of misspent time and wasted hours? Eternity only will answer. The ceaseless flight of the seasons is to me a very solemn thought ; and yet why do we not strive to make a better improvement of them? With how much emphasis the poet has said, ' We take no note of time but from its loss. 'T were wise in man to give it then a tongue. Pay no moment but in just purchase of its worth, and what its worth ask death-beds. They can tell. Part with it as with life reluctantly.' Then we have higher authority than that of man for the improvement of our time. For God has said, ' Work while the day lasts, for the night is coming in the which no man can work.' Let us strive together to part with time more reluctantly, to watch the pinions of the fleeting moment until they are dim in the distance, and the new-coming moment claims our attention. I have perfect confidence in God and His promises, and yet I know not why I feel that the world holds a predominant place in my affections. . . . Your affectionate friend,

Emily E. D.

Numerous postscripts are appended, as usually : —

I have really suffered from the heat the last week. I think it remarkable that we should have such weather in September. There were over one hundred deaths in Boston last week, a great many of them owing to the heat. Mr Taylor, our old teacher, was in Amherst at Commencement time. Oh, I do love Mr Taylor. It seems so like old times to meet Miss Adams and Mr Taylor together again. I could hardly refrain from singing, ' Auld Lang Syne.' It seemed so very *à propos*. Have you forgotten the memorable ride we all took with Mr Taylor, ' Long, long ago '? . . . Austin entered college last Commencement. Only think ! I have a brother who has the honor to be a Freshman ! Will you not promise me that you will come to Commencement when he graduates? Do ! Please ! I have altered very much since you were here. I am now very tall, and wear long dresses nearly. Do you believe we shall know each other when we meet? Don't forget to write soon.   E.

Sabbath Eve, 1846.

My dear A.,— When I last wrote you I was in Boston, where I spent a delightful visit of four weeks. I returned home about the middle of September in very good health and spirits, for which it seems to me I cannot be sufficiently grateful to the Giver of all mercies. I expected to go into the Academy upon my return home, but as I stayed longer than I expected to, and as the school had already commenced, I made up my mind to remain at home during the fall term and pursue my studies the winter term, which commences a week after Thanksgiving. I kept my good resolution for once in my life, and have been sewing, practising upon the piano, and assisting mother in household affairs. I am anticipating the commencement of the next term with a great deal of pleasure, for I have been an exile from school two terms on account of my health, and you know what it is to 'love school.' Miss Adams is with us now, and will remain through the winter, and we have an excellent Principal in the person of Mr Leonard Humphrey, who was the last valedictorian. We now have a fine school. I thank you a thousand times for your long and affectionate letter. . . . I found a quantity of sewing waiting with open arms to embrace me, or rather for me to embrace it, and I could hardly give myself up to 'Nature's sweet restorer,' for the ghosts of out-of-order garments crying for vengeance upon my defenceless head.   However, I am happy to inform you, my dear friend, that I have nearly finished my sewing for winter, and will answer all the letters which you shall deem worthy to send so naughty a girl as myself, at short notice. . . .

Write soon.   Your affectionate

EMILY E. D.

[March 15, 1847.]

Sabbath Eve, 1847.

EVER DEAR A.,—. . . We have spent our vacation of a fortnight, and school has commenced again since you wrote me.   I go this term, and am studying Algebra, Euclid, Ecclesiastical History, and reviewing Arithmetic again to be upon the safe side of things next autumn.   We have a delightful school this term under the instruction of our former principals, and Miss R. Woodbridge, daughter of Rev. Dr W. of Hadley, for preceptress.   We all love her very much.   Perhaps a slight description of her might be interesting to my dear A.   She is tall and rather slender, but finely proportioned, has a most witching pair of blue eyes, rich brown hair, delicate complexion, cheeks which vie with the opening rose-bud, teeth like pearls, dimples which come and go like the ripples in yonder little merry brook, and then she is so affectionate and lovely. Forgive my glowing description, for you know I am always in love with my teachers.   Yet, much as we love her, it seems lonely and strange without 'our dear Miss Adams.' I suppose you know that she has left Amherst, not again to return as a teacher. It is indeed true that she is to be married. Are you not astonished? Nothing was known but that she was to return to the school, until a few days before she left for Syracuse, where she has gone to make her 'wedding gear.' She is to be married the first of next April, to a very respectable lawyer in Conway, Massachusetts. She seemed to be very happy in anticipation of her future prospects, and I hope she will realize all her fond hopes. I cannot bear to think that she will never more wield the sceptre and sit upon the throne in our venerable schoolhouse, and yet I am glad she is going to have a home of her own, and a kind companion to take life's journey with her. I am delighted that she is to live so near us, for we can ride up and see her often. You cannot imagine how much I enjoyed your description of your Christmas fête at Miss Campbell's. How magnificent the 'Christmas tree' must have been, and what a grand time you must have had, so many of you! Oh!!

I had a great many presents, Christmas and New Year's holidays, both, but we had no such celebration of the former which you describe. . . . Do write me soon — a long letter — and tell me how soon you are coming, and how long we can keep you when you come. Your affectionate

EMILY E. DICKINSON.

MT HOLYOKE SEMINARY, Nov. 6, 1847.

MY DEAR A., — I am really at Mount Holyoke
Seminary, and this is to be my home for a long year.
Your affectionate letter was joyfully received, and I
wish that this might make you as happy as yours did
me. It has been nearly six weeks since I left home,
and that is a longer time than I was ever away from
home before now. I was very homesick for a few
days, and it seemed to me I could not live here.
But I am now contented and quite happy, if I can
be happy when absent from my dear home and
friends. You may laugh at the idea that I cannot
be happy when away from home, but you must
remember that I have a very dear home and that
this is my first trial in the way of absence for any
length of time in my life. As you desire it, I will
give you a full account of myself since I first left the
paternal roof. I came to South Hadley six weeks ago
next Thursday. I was much fatigued with the ride,
and had a severe cold besides, which prevented me
from commencing my examinations until the next
day, when I began. I finished them in three days,
and found them about what I had anticipated, though
the old scholars say they are more strict than they
ever have been before. As you can easily imagine,
I was much delighted to finish without failures, and
I came to the conclusion then, that I should not be
at all homesick, but the reaction left me as homesick
a girl as it is not usual to see. I am now quite con-

tented and am very much occupied in reviewing the Junior studies, as I wish to enter the middle class. The school is very large, and though quite a number have left, on account of finding the examinations more difficult than they anticipated, yet there are nearly 300 now. Perhaps you know that Miss Lyon is raising her standard of scholarship a good deal, on account of the number of applicants this year, and she makes the examinations more severe than usual.

You cannot imagine how trying they are, because if we cannot go through them all in a specified time, we are sent home. I cannot be too thankful that I got through as soon as I did, and I am sure that I never would endure the suspense which I endured during those three days again for all the treasures of the world.

I room with my cousin Emily, who is a Senior. She is an excellent room-mate, and does all in her power to make me happy. You can imagine how pleasant a good room-mate is, for you have been away to school so much. Everything is pleasant and happy here, and I think I could be no happier at any other school away from home. Things seem much more like home than I anticipated, and the teachers are all very kind and affectionate to us. They call on us frequently and urge us to return their calls, and when we do, we always receive a cordial welcome from them. I will tell you my order of time for the day, as you were so kind as to give

me yours. At 6 o'clock we all rise. We breakfast
at 7. Our study hours begin at 8. At 9 we all meet
in Seminary Hall for devotions. At 10¼ I recite a
review of Ancient History, in connection with which
we read Goldsmith and Grimshaw. At 11, I recite
a lesson in Pope's *Essay on Man*, which is merely
transposition. At 12 I practise calisthenics, and at
12¼ read until dinner, which is at 12½, and after
dinner, from 1½ until 2, I sing in Seminary Hall.
From 2¾ until 3¾ I practise upon the piano. At 3¾
I go to Sections, where we give in all our accounts
for the day, including absence, tardiness, communi-
cations, breaking silent study hours, receiving company in our rooms, and ten thousand other things
which I will not take time or place to mention. At
4½ we go into Seminary Hall and receive advice from
Miss Lyon in the form of a lecture. We have supper
at 6, and silent study hours from then until the retiring bell, which rings at 8¾, but the tardy bell does
not ring until 9¾, so that we don't often obey the
first warning to retire. Unless we have a good and
reasonable excuse for failure upon any of the items
that I mentioned above, they are recorded and a
black mark stands against our names. As you can
easily imagine, we do not like very well to get 'exceptions,' as they are called scientifically here.

My domestic work is not difficult and consists
in carrying the knives from the first tier of tables
at morning and noon, and at night washing and
wiping the same quantity of knives. I am quite

well and hope to be able to spend the year here,
free from sickness. You have probably heard many
reports of the food here; and if so, I can tell you
that I have yet seen nothing corresponding to my
ideas on that point from what I have heard. Everything is wholesome and abundant and much nicer
than I should imagine could be provided for almost
300 girls. We have also a great variety upon our
tables and frequent changes. One thing is certain,
and that is, that Miss Lyon and all the teachers
seem to consult our comfort and happiness in
everything they do, and you know that is pleasant.
When I left home I did not think I should find a
companion or a dear friend in all the multitude. I
expected to find rough and uncultivated manners,
and, to be sure, I have found some of that stamp,
but on the whole, there is an ease and grace, a desire
to make one another happy, which delights and at
the same time surprises me very much. I find no
Abby nor Abiah nor Mary, but I love many of the
girls. Austin came to see me when I had been here
about two weeks, and brought Viny and A. I need
not tell you how delighted I was to see them all, nor
how happy it made me to hear them say that 'they
were *so lonely*.' It is a sweet feeling to know that
you are missed and that your memory is precious at
home. This week, on Wednesday, I was at my window, when I happened to look towards the hotel
and saw father and mother, walking over here as
dignified as you please. I need not tell you that I

danced and clapped my hands, and flew to meet them, for you can imagine how I felt. I will only ask you, do you love your parents? They wanted to surprise me, and for that reason did not let me know they were coming. I could not bear to have them go, but go they must, and so I submitted in sadness. Only to think that in 2½ weeks I shall be at my *own dear home* again. You will probably go home at Thanksgiving time, and we can rejoice with each other.

You don't [know] how I laughed at your description of your introduction to Daniel Webster, and I read that part of your letter to cousin Emily. You must feel quite proud of the acquaintance, and will not, I hope, be vain in consequence. However, you don't know Governor Briggs, and I do, so you are no better off than I. . . . A., you must write me often, and I shall write you as often as I have time. . . .

From your affectionate

Emily E. D.

MT HOLYOKE FEMALE SEMINARY, Jan. 17, 1848.

MY DEAR A., — Your welcome epistle found me upon the eve of going home, and it is needless to say very happy. We all went home on Wednesday before Thanksgiving, and a stormy day it was, but the storm must not be in our way, so we tried to make the best of it and look as cheerful as we could. Many of the girls went very early in the morning in order to reach home the same day, and when we all sat down to the breakfast table, it seemed lonely enough to see so many places vacant. After breakfast, as we were not required to keep all the family rules, a number of us met together at one of the windows in the Hall to watch for our friends, whom we were constantly expecting. No morning of my life ever passed so slowly to me, and it really seemed to me they never were coming, so impatiently did I wait their arrival. At last, almost tired out, I spied a carriage in the distance, and surely Austin was in it. You, who have been away so much, can easily imagine my delight and will not laugh, when I tell you how I dashed downstairs and almost frightened my dignified brother out of his senses. All was ready in a moment or less than a moment, and cousin Emily and myself, not for-getting the driver, were far on our way towards home. The rain fell in torrents and the wind howled around the sides of the mountain over our heads, and the brooks below, filled by the rain, rushed along their pebbly beds almost frightfully, yet nothing daunted, we rode swiftly along, and soon the colleges and the spire of our venerable meeting-house rose to my delighted vision.

Never did Amherst look more lovely to me, and gratitude rose in my heart to God, for granting me such a safe return to my *own dear home.* Soon the carriage stopped in front of our own house, and all were at the door to welcome the returned one, from mother, with tears in her eyes, down to pussy, who

tried to look as gracious as was becoming her dignity.
Oh, A., it was the first meeting, as it had been the
first separation, and it was a joyful one to all of us.
The storm did not at all subside that night, but in
the morning I was waked by the glorious sunshine
[it] self, staring full in my face. We went to church
in the morning and listened to an excellent sermon
from our own minister, Mr Colton. At noon we
returned and had a nice dinner, which, you well
know, cannot be dispensed with on Thanksgiving
day. We had several calls in the afternoon, and
had four invitations out for the evening. Of course
we could not accept them all, much to my sorrow,
but decided to make two visits. At about 7 o'clock
father, mother, Austin, Viny, cousin Emily, and myself to bring up the rear, went down to Professor
Warner's, where we spent an hour delightfully with
a few friends, and then bidding them good eve, we
young folks went down to Mrs S. M.'s, accompanied
by *sister Mary*. There was quite a company of
young people assembled when we arrived, and after
we had played many games we had, in familiar terms,
a 'candy scrape.' We enjoyed the evening much,
and returned not until the clock pealed out, 'Remember ten o'clock, my dear, remember ten o'clock.'
After our return, father wishing to hear the piano,
I, like an obedient daughter, played and sang a few
tunes, much to his apparent gratification. We then
retired, and the next day and the next were as happily spent as the eventful Thanksgiving day itself.

You will probably think me foolish thus to give you an inventory of my time while at home, but I did enjoy so much in those short four days that I wanted you to know and enjoy it too. Monday came so soon, and with it came a carriage to our door, and amidst tears falling thick and fast away I went again. Slowly and sadly dragged a few of the days after my return to the Seminary, and I was very homesick, but 'after a storm there comes a calm,' and so it was in my case. My sorrows were soon lost in study, and I again felt happy, if happiness there can be away from 'home, sweet home.'

Our term closes this week on Thursday, and Friday I hope to see home and friends once more. I have studied hard this term, and aside from my delight at going home, there is a sweetness in approaching rest to me. This term is the longest in the year, and I would not wish to live it over again, I can assure you. I love this Seminary, and all the teachers are bound strongly to my heart by ties of affection. There are many sweet girls here, and dearly do I love some new faces, but I have not yet found the place of a *few* dear ones filled, nor would I wish it to be here. I am now studying Silliman's Chemistry and Cutter's Physiology, in both of which I am much interested. We finish Physiology before this term closes, and are to be examined in it at the spring examinations, about five weeks after the commencement of the next term. I already begin to dread that time, for an examination in Mount Holyoke Seminary is rather more public than in our old academy, and a failure would be more disgraceful then, I opine ; but I hope, to use my father's own words, 'that I shall not disgrace myself.' What are you studying now? You did not mention that item in your last letters to me, and consequently I am quite in the dark as regards your progress in those affairs. All I can say is, that I hope you will not leave poor me far behind. . . .

Your affectionate sister,

EMILY E. DICKINSON.

P. S. Our Section have commenced reading compositions, and we read once in a month, during which time we write two.

Intellectual brilliancy of an individual type was already at seventeen her distinguishing characteristic, and nothing of the recluse was yet apparent. Traditions of extraordinary compositions still remain ; and it is certain that each was an epoch for those who heard, whether teachers or pupils. An old friend and schoolmate of Emily tells me that she was always surrounded by a group of girls at recess, to hear her strange and intensely funny stories, invented upon the spot.

MT HOLYOKE FEMALE SEMINARY, May 16, 1848.

MY DEAR A., — You must forgive me, indeed you must, that I have so long delayed to write you, and I doubt not you will when I give you all my reasons for so doing. You know it is customary for the first page to be occupied with apologies, and I must not depart from the beaten track for one of my own imagining. . . . I had not been very well all winter, but had not written home about it, lest the folks should take me home. During the week following examinations, a friend from Amherst came over and spent a week with me, and when that friend returned home, father and mother were duly notified of the state of my health. Have you so treacherous a friend?

Not knowing that I was to be reported at home, you can imagine my amazement and consternation when Saturday of the same week Austin arrived in full sail, with orders from head-quarters to bring me home at all events. At first I had recourse to words, and a desperate battle with those weapons was waged for a few moments, between my *Sophomore* brother and myself. Finding words of no avail, I next resorted to tears. But woman's tears are of little avail, and I am sure mine flowed in vain. As you can imagine, Austin was victorious, and poor, defeated I was led off in triumph. You must not imbibe the idea from what I have said that I do not love home — far from it. But I could not bear to leave teachers and companions before the close of the term and go home to be dosed and receive the physician daily, and take warm drinks and be condoled with on the state of health in general by all the old ladies in town.

Have n't I given a ludicrous account of going home sick from a boarding-school? Father is quite a hand to give medicine, especially if it is not desirable to the patient, and I was dosed for about a month after my return home, without any mercy, till at last out of mere pity my cough went away, and I had quite a season of peace. Thus I remained at home until the close of the term, comforting my parents by my presence, and instilling many a lesson of wisdom into the budding intellect of my only sister. I had almost forgotten to tell you that I went on with my studies at home, and kept up with my class. Last Thursday our vacation closed, and on Friday morn, midst the weeping of friends, crowing of roosters, and singing of birds, I again took my departure from home. Five days have now passed · since we returned to Holyoke, and they have passed very slowly. Thoughts of home and friends 'come crowding thick and fast, like lightnings from the mountain cloud,' and it seems very desolate.

Father has decided not to send me to Holyoke another year, so this is my *last term*. Can it be possible that I have been here almost a year? It startles me when I really think of the advantages I

have had, and I fear I have not improved them as
I ought.   But many an hour has fled with its report
to heaven, and what has been the tale of me? . . .
How glad I am that spring has come, and how it
calms my mind when wearied with study to walk out
in the green fields and beside the pleasant streams
in which South Hadley is rich !   There are not many
wild flowers near, for the girls have driven them to
a distance, and we are obliged to walk quite a distance to find them, but they repay us by their sweet
smiles and fragrance.

The older I grow, the more do I love spring and
spring flowers.   Is it so with you?   While at home
there were several pleasure parties of which I was
a member, and in our rambles we found many and
beautiful children of spring, which I will mention
and see if you have found them, — the trailing arbutus, adder's tongue, yellow violets, liver-leaf, blood-
root, and many other smaller flowers.

What are you reading now?   I have little time to
read when I am here, but while at home I had a feast
in the reading line, I can assure you.   Two or three
of them I will mention : *Evangeline, The Princess,
The Maiden Aunt, The Epicurean,* and *The Twins
and Heart* by Tupper, complete the list.   Am not
I a pedant for telling you what I have been reading?   Have you forgotten your visit at Amherst last
summer, and what delightful times we had?   I have
not, and I hope you will come and make another
and a longer, when I get home from Holyoke.

Father wishes to have me at home a year, and then he will probably send me away again, where I know not. . . .

> Ever your own affectionate
>
> EMILIE E. DICKINSON.

P. S.   My studies for this series are Astronomy and Rhetoric, which take me through to the Senior studies.   What are you studying now, if you are in school, and do you attend to music?   I practise only one hour a day this term.

Although nearly two years elapse between the last letter and the following, the handwriting is quite unaltered, being still exceedingly small and clear, and averaging twenty words to a line.

AMHERST, Jan. 29, 1850.

VERY DEAR A., — The folks have all gone away; they thought that they left me alone, and contrived things to amuse me should they stay long, and *I* be lonely.   Lonely, indeed, — they did n't look, and they could n't have seen if they had, who should bear me company.   *Three* here, instead of *one*, would n't it scare them?   A curious trio, part earthly and part spiritual two of us, the other, all heaven, and no earth.   *God* is sitting here, looking into my very soul to see if I think right thoughts. Yet I am not afraid, for I try to be right and good ; and He knows every one of my struggles. He looks very gloriously, and everything bright seems dull beside Him ; and I don't dare to look directly at Him for fear I shall die.   Then *you* are here, dressed in that quiet black gown and cap, — that funny little cap I used to laugh at you about, — and you don't appear to be thinking about anything in particular, — not in one of your *breaking-dish* moods, I take it.   You seem aware that I'm writing you, and are amused, I should think, at any such friendly manifestation when you are already present.   *Success*, however, even in making a fool of myself, isn't to be despised ; so I shall persist in writing, and you may in laughing at me, — if you are fully aware of the value of time as regards your immortal spirit.   I can't say that I advise you to laugh ; but if you are punished, and I warned you, that can be no business of mine.   So I fold up my arms, and leave you to fate — may it deal very kindly with you !   The trinity winds up with me, as you may have surmised, and I certainly would n't be at the fag-end but for civility to you. This self-sacrificing spirit will be the ruin of me !

I am occupied principally with a cold just now, and the dear creature *will* have so much attention that my time slips away amazingly.   It has heard *so* much of New Englanders, of their kind attentions to strangers, that it's come all the way from the Alps to determine the truth of the tale.   It says the half was n't told it, and I begin to be afraid it

was n't. Only think — came all the way from that
distant Switzerland to find what was the truth! Neither
husband, protector, nor friend accompanied it, and
so utter a state of loneliness gives friends if nothing
else. You are dying of curiosity; let me arrange that
pillow to make your exit easier. I stayed at home
all Saturday afternoon, and treated some disagree-
able people who insisted upon calling here as toler-
ably as I could; when evening shades began to fall, I
turned upon my heel, and walked. Attracted by
the gayety visible in the street, I still kept walking
till a little creature pounced upon a thin shawl I
wore, and commenced riding. I stopped, and
begged the creature to alight, as I was fatigued
already, and quite unable to assist others. It
would n't get down, and commenced talking to
itself: 'Can't be New England — must have made
some mistake — disappointed in my reception — don't
agree with accounts. Oh, what a world of decep-
tion and fraud! Marm, will you tell me the name
of this country — it 's Asia Minor, is n't it? I
intended to stop in New England.' By this time
I was so completely exhausted that I made no further effort to rid me of my load, and travelled home
at a moderate jog, paying no attention whatever to
it, got into the house, threw off both bonnet and
shawl, and out flew my tormentor, and putting both
arms around my neck, began to kiss me immoder-
ately, and express so much love it completely
bewildered me. Since then it has slept in my bed,

eaten from my plate, lived with me everywhere, and will tag me through life for all I know. I think I 'll wake first, and get out of bed, and leave it; but early or late, it is dressed before me, and sits on the side of the bed looking right into my face with such a comical expression it almost makes me laugh in spite of myself. I can't call it interesting, but it certainly *is* curious, has two peculiarities which would quite win your heart, — a huge pocket-handkerchief and a very red nose. The first seems so very *abundant*, it gives you the idea of independence and prosperity in business. The last brings up the 'jovial bowl, my boys,' and such an association 's worth the having. If it *ever* gets tired of *me*, I will forward it to *you* — you would love it for *my* sake, if not for its own; it will tell you some queer stories about me, — how I sneezed so loud one night that the family thought the last trump was sounding, and climbed into the currant-bushes to get out of the way; how the rest of the people, arrayed in long night-gowns, folded their arms, and were waiting; but this is a wicked story, — it can tell some better ones. Now, my dear friend, let me tell you that these last thoughts are fictions, — vain imaginations to lead astray foolish young women. They are flowers of speech; they both make and tell deliberate falsehoods; avoid them as the snake, and turn aside as from the rattle-snake, and I don't *think* you will be harmed. Honestly, though, a snake-bite is a serious matter,

and there can't be too much said or done about
it. The big serpent bites the deepest; and we get
so accustomed to its bites that we don't mind
about them. 'Verily I say unto you, fear *him.*'
Won't you read some work upon snakes? — I have
a real anxiety for you. *I* love those little green
ones that slide around by your shoes in the grass,
and make it rustle with their elbows; they are
rather my favorites on the whole; but I would n't
influence *you* for the world. There is an air of
misanthropy about the striped snake that will commend itself at once to your taste, — there is no
monotony about it — but we will more of this again.
Something besides severe colds and serpents, and
we will try to find *that* something. It can't be
a garden, can it? or a strawberry-bed, which rather
belongs to a garden; nor it can't be a schoolhouse, nor an attorney-at-law. Oh, dear! I don't
know what it is. Love for the absent don't *sound*
like it; but try it, and see how it goes.

I miss you very much indeed; think of you at
night when the world's nodding, nid, nid, nodding
— think of you in the daytime when the cares of the
world, and its toils, and its continual vexations
choke up the love for friends in some of our
hearts; remember your warnings sometimes — try
to do as you told me sometimes — and sometimes
conclude it's no use to try; then my heart says it
is, and new trial is followed by disappointment
again. I wondered, when you had gone, why we

did n't talk more, — it was n't for want of a subject; it never *could be* for *that*. Too many, perhaps, — such a crowd of people that nobody heard the speaker, and all went away discontented. You astonished me in the outset, perplexed me in the continuance, and wound up in a grand snarl I shall be all my pilgrimage unravelling. Rather a dismal prospect certainly; but 'it's always the darkest the hour before day,' and this earlier sunset promises an earlier rise — a sun in splendor — and glory, flying out of its purple nest. Would n't you love to see God's bird, when it first tries its wings? If you were here I would tell you something — several somethings — which have happened since you went away; but time and space, as usual, oppose themselves, and I put my treasures away till 'we two meet again.' The hope that I shall continue in love towards you, and *vice versa*, will sustain me till then. If you are thinking soon to go away, and to show your face no more, just inform me, will you? I would have the 'long, lingering look,' which you cast behind, — it would be an invaluable addition to my treasures, and 'keep your memory green.' 'Lord, keep all our memories green,' and help on our affection, and tie the 'link that doth us bind' in a tight .bow-knot that will keep it from separation, and stop us from growing old; if that is impossible, make old age pleasant to us, put its arms around us kindly, and when we go home, let that home be called heaven.

Your very sincere and *wicked* friend,

EMILY E. DICKINSON.ˈ

I have n't thanked you for your letter yet, but not for want of gratitude. I will do so *now* most sincerely, most heartily — gladly and gratefully. You will write me another soon, that I may have *four right* feelings again! They don't come for the asking. I have been introducing you to me in this letter so far; we will traffic in 'joys' and 'sorrows' some other day. Colds make one very carnal, and the spirit is always afraid of them. You will excuse all mistakes in view of ignorance; all sin, in view of 'the fall;' all want of friendly affection, in the sight of the verse, 'The deepest stream the stillest runs;' and other general deficiencies, on the ground of universal incapacity! Here is surely room for charity, and the heavenly visitor would n't have come but for these faults. 'No loss without a gain.' I called to see your cousins an evening since; they were well, and evidently delighted to see one another — and us.

When your letter came, I had two Western cousins — now at South Hadley Seminary — staying their vacation with me. They took an unbounded delight in a sentence I read them; and to pay for it, send you their love.

In the following letter appear farther traces of the later and almost invariable custom of using dashes, instead of conventional punctuation. These, however, will not be given generally. In printing her poems it was found necessary to employ usual punctuation, in order that the meaning should be more easily apprehended; and in the letters the same system, often for the same reason, has been adopted.

AMHERST, May 7, 1850.

DEAR REMEMBERED, — The circumstances under which I write you this morning are at once glorious, afflicting, and beneficial, — glorious in *ends*, afflicting in *means*, and beneficial, I trust, in *both*. Twin loaves of bread have just been born into the world under my auspices, — fine children, the image of their mother; and here, my dear friend, is the *glory*.

On the lounge, asleep, lies my sick mother, suffering intensely from acute neuralgia, except at a moment like this, when kind sleep draws near, and beguiles her, — here is the *affliction*.

I need not draw the beneficial inference, — the good I myself derive, the winning the spirit of patience, the genial housekeeping influence stealing over my mind and soul, — you know all these things I would say, and will seem to suppose they are written, when indeed they are only thought.

On Sunday my mother was taken, had been perfectly well before, and could remember no possible imprudence which should have induced the disease. Everything has been done, and though we think her gradually throwing it off, she still has much suffering. I have always neglected the culinary arts, but attend to them now from necessity, and from a desire to make everything pleasant for father and Austin. Sickness makes desolation, and the day is dark and dreary; but health will come back, I hope, and light hearts and smiling faces. We are sick hardly ever at home, and don't know what to do when it comes, — wrinkle our little brows, and stamp with our little feet, and our tiny souls get angry, and command it to go away. Mrs Brown will be glad to see it, — old ladies expect to die; 'as for *us*, the young and active, with all longings "for the strife," *we* to perish by the roadside, weary with the "march of life" — no, no, my dear "Father Mortality," get out of the way if you please; we will call if we ever want you. Good-morning, sir! ah, good-morning!'

When I am not at work, I sit by the side of mother, provide for her little wants, and try to cheer and encourage her. I ought to be glad and grateful that I *can* do anything now, but I do feel so very lonely, and so anxious to have her cured. I have n't repined but once, and you shall know all the why. At noon . . . I heard a well-known rap, and a friend I love *so* dearly came and asked me to ride in the woods, the sweet, still woods, — and I wanted to exceedingly. I told him I could not go, and he said he was disappointed, he wanted me very much. Then the tears came into my eyes, though I tried to choke them back, and he said I *could* and *should* go, and it seemed to me unjust. Oh, I struggled with great temptation, and it cost me much of denial; but I think in the end I conquered, — not a glorious victory, where you hear the rolling drum, but a kind of a helpless victory, where triumph would come of itself, faintest music, weary soldiers, nor a waving flag, nor a long, loud shout. I had read of Christ's temptations, and how they were like our own, only he did n't sin; I wondered if *one* was like mine, and whether it made him angry. I could n't make up my mind; do you think he ever did?

I went cheerfully round my work, humming a little air till mother had gone to sleep, then cried with all my might — seemed to think I was much abused — that this wicked world was unworthy such devoted and terrible suffering — and came to my various senses in great dudgeon at life, and time, and love for affliction and anguish.

What shall we do, my darling, when trial grows more and more, when 'the dim, lone light expires, and it 's dark, so very dark, and we wander, and know not where, and cannot get out of the forest — whose is the hand to help us, and to lead,

and forever guide us; they talk of a 'Jesus of
Nazareth' — will you tell me if it be he? . . .

It's Friday, my dear A., and that in another week,
yet my mission is unfulfilled — and you so sadly
neglected, and don't know the reason why. Where
do you think I've strayed, and from what new
errand returned? I have come from 'to and fro,
and walking up and down' the same place that
Satan hailed from, when God asked him where
he'd been; but not to illustrate further, I tell you
I have been dreaming, dreaming a *golden* dream,
with eyes all the while wide open, and I guess it's
almost morning; and besides, I have been at work,
providing the 'food that perisheth,' scaring the
timorous dust, and being obedient and kind. I am
yet the Queen of the Court, if regalia be dust and
dirt, have three loyal subjects, whom I'd rather
relieve from service. Mother is still an invalid,
though a partially restored one; father and Austin
still clamor for food; and I, like a martyr, am feed-
ing them. Wouldn't you love to see me in these
bonds of great despair, looking around my kitchen,
and praying for kind deliverance, and declaring by
'Omai's beard' I never was in such plight? *My*
kitchen, I think I called it — God forbid that it
was, or shall be, my own — God keep me from what
they call *households*, except that bright one of
'faith'!

Don't be afraid of my imprecations — they never
did any one harm, and they make me feel so cool,

and so very much more comfortable! . . . I
presume you are loving your mother, and loving
the stranger and wanderer — visiting the poor and
afflicted, and reaping whole fields of blessings —
save me a little sheaf, only a very little one! Remember and care for me sometimes, and scatter a
fragrant flower in this wilderness life of mine by
writing me, and by not forgetting, and by lingering
longer in prayer, that the Father may bless one more!

Your affectionate friend,

EMILY.

Mr Humphrey, spoken of in the following
letter, is the same friend of whom Emily had
already written (page 24); he graduated from
Amherst as valedictorian in 1846, being subse-
quently Principal of the well-known Amherst
Academy, and still later a theological student
at Andover, and tutor in Amherst College.
His sudden death, November 30, 1850, caused
much grief to his many friends, who admired his
polished scholarship and lovable personality.

[Amherst, January 2, 1851.]

Tuesday Evening.

I write A. to-night, because it is cool and quiet,
and I can forget the toil and care of the feverish
day, and then I am *selfish* too, because I am feeling
lonely; some of my friends are gone, and some of
my friends are sleeping — sleeping the churchyard

sleep — the hour of evening is sad — it was once my study hour — my master has gone to rest, and the open leaf of the book, and the scholar at school *alone*, make the tears come, and I cannot brush them away; I would not if I could, for they are the only tribute I can pay the departed Humphrey.

You have stood by the grave before; I have walked there sweet summer evenings and read the names on the stones, and wondered who would come and give me the same memorial; but I never have laid my friends there, and forgot that they too must die; this is my first affliction, and indeed 't is hard to bear it. To those bereaved so often that home is no more here, and whose communion with friends is had only in prayers, there must be much to hope for, but when the unreconciled spirit has nothing left but God, that spirit is lone indeed. I don't think there will be any sunshine, or any singing-birds in the spring that 's coming. . . . I will try not to say any more — my rebellious thoughts are many, and the friend I love and trust in has much *now* to forgive. I wish I were somebody else — I would pray the prayer of the 'Pharisee,' but I am a poor little 'Publican.' 'Son of David,' look down on me!

'T was a great while ago when you wrote me, I remember the leaves were falling — and *now* there are falling snows; who maketh the two to differ — are not leaves the brethren of snows?

Then it *can't* be a great while since then, though I verily thought it *was;* we are not so young as we

once were, and time seems to be growing long.   I
dream of being a grandame, and banding my silver
hairs, and I seem to be quite submissive to the
thought of growing old ; no doubt you ride rocking-
horses in your present as in young sleeps — quite
a pretty contrast indeed, of me braiding my own
gray hairs, and my friend at play with her childhood,
a pair of decayed old ladies !   Where *are* you, my
antique friend, or my very dear and young one —
just as you please to please — it *may* seem quite
a presumption that I address you at all, knowing
not if you habit here, or if my 'bird has flown' in
which world her wing is folded.   When I think of
the friends I love, and the little while we may
dwell here, and then 'we go away,' I have a yearning feeling, a desire eager and anxious lest any
be stolen away, so that I cannot behold them.   I
would have you here, all here, where I can *see* you,
and *hear* you, and where I can say 'Oh, no,' if the
'Son of Man' ever 'cometh' !

It is not enough, now and then, at long and uncer-
tain intervals to hear you 're alive and well.   I do not
care for the body, I love the timid soul, the blush-
ing, shrinking soul ; it hides, for it is afraid, and the
bold, obtrusive body —   Pray, marm, did you call
me ? We are very small, A. — I think we grow still
smaller — this tiny, insect life the portal to another ;
it seems strange — strange indeed.   I 'm afraid we
are all unworthy, yet we shall 'enter in.'

I can think of no other way than for you, my dear

girl, to come here — we are growing away from each
other, and talk even now like strangers.   To forget
the 'meum and teum,' *dearest* friends must meet
sometimes, and then comes the 'bond of the spirit'
which, if I am correct, is 'unity.'

. . . You are growing wiser than I am, and nip-
ping in the bud fancies which I let blossom — per-
chance to bear no fruit, or if plucked, I may find it
bitter.   The shore is safer, A., but I love to buffet
the sea — I can count the bitter wrecks here in these
pleasant waters, and hear the murmuring winds, but
oh, I love the danger!   You are learning control and
firmness.   Christ Jesus will love you more.   I'm
afraid he don't love me *any!* . . . Write when you
will, my friend, and forget all amiss herein, for as
these few imperfect words to the full communion
of spirits, so this small giddy life to the *better*, the
life eternal, and that *we* may live this life, and be
filled with this true communion, I shall not cease to
pray.   E.

[August, 1851.]

Tuesday Evening.

'Yet a little while I am with you, and again a little while and I am *not* with you,' because you go to
your mother! . . . But the virtue of the text consists in this, my dear, that 'if I *go*, I come again,
and ye shall be with me where I am;' that is to say,
that if you come in November, you shall be mine,
and I shall be thine, and so on, *vice versa*, until *ad*

infinitum, which is n't a great way off. While I think of it, my dear friend, and we are upon these subjects, allow me to remark that you have the funniest manner of popping into town, and the most lamentable manner of popping out again, of any one I know. It really becomes to me a matter of serious moment, this propensity of yours concerning your female friends — the 'morning cloud and the early dew' are not more evanescent.

I think it was Tuesday evening that we were so amused by the oratorical feats of three or four young gentlemen. I remember I sat by you and took great satisfaction in such seat and society — I remember further our mutual good-nights, our promises to meet again, to tell each other tales of our own heart and life, to seek and find each other after so long a time of distant separation. I can hardly realize that these are recollections, that our happy to-day joins the great band of yesterdays and marches on to the dead — too quickly flown, my bird, for me to satisfy me that you *did* sit and sing beneath my chamber window! I only went out once after the time I saw you — the morning of Mr Beecher I looked for you in vain. I discovered your Palmer cousins, but if you indeed were there, it must have been in a form to my gross sense impalpable. I was disappointed. I had been hoping much a little visit from you; when will the hour be that we shall sit together and talk of what we were and what we are and may be — with the shutters closed, dear

A., and the balmiest little breeze stealing in at the
window? I love those little fancies, yet I would
love them more were they not quite so fanciful as
they have seemed to be. I have fancied so many
times, and so many times gone home to find it was
only fancy, that I am half afraid to hope for what I
long for. It would seem, my dear A., that out of
all the moments crowding this little world, a *few*
might be vouchsafed to spend with those we love —
a separated hour, an hour more pure and true than
ordinary hours, when we could pause a moment,
before we journey on. We had a pleasant time talking the other morning — had I known it was all
my portion, mayhap I 'd improved it more, but it
never 'll come back again to try, whether or no.
Don't you think sometimes these brief, imperfect
meetings have a tale to tell — perhaps but for the
sorrow which accompanies them we should not be
reminded of brevity and change, and should build
the dwelling earthward whose site is in the skies —
perhaps the treasure here would be too dear a treasure could n't 'the moth corrupt, and the thief break
through and steal;' and this makes me think how
I found a little moth in my stores the other day,
a very subtle moth that had, in ways and manners to me and mine unknown, contrived to hide
itself in a favorite worsted basket — how long my
little treasure-house had furnished an arena for its
destroying labors it is not mine to tell; it had an
errand there — I trust it fulfilled its mission; it

taught me, dear A., to have no treasure here, or rather it tried to tell me in its little mothy way of another enduring treasure the robber cannot steal, nor time waste away. How many a lesson learned from lips of such tiny teachers — don't it make you think of the Bible, 'not many mighty, nor wise'?

You met our dear Sarah T. after I saw you here. Her sweet face is the same as in those happy school-days — and in vain I search for wrinkles brought on by many cares ; we all love Sarah dearly, and shall try to do all in our power to make her visit happy. Is n't it very remarkable that in so many years Sarah has changed so little — not that she has stood still, but has made such *peaceful* progress — her thoughts, though they are older, have all the charm of youth — have not yet lost their freshness, their innocence and peace ; she seems so pure in heart, so sunny and serene, like some sweet lark or robin, ever soaring and singing. I have not seen her much — I want to see her more — she speaks often of *you*, and with a warm affection. I hope no change or time shall blight those loves of ours, I would bear them all in my arms to my home in the glorious heaven and say, 'Here am I, my Father, and those whom thou hast given me.' If the life which is to come is better than dwelling *here*, and angels are there and our friends are glorified and are singing there and praising there, need we fear to go when spirits beyond wait for us? I was meaning to see you more and talk about such things with you —   I

want to know your views and your eternal feelings
— how things beyond are to you — oh, there is much
to speak of in meeting one you love, and it always
seems to me that I might have spoken more, and I
almost always think that what we found to say might
have been left unspoken.

Shall it *always* be so, A.? Is there no longer day
given for our communion with the spirits of our
love? Writing is brief and fleeting — conversation
will come again, yet if it *will*, it hastes and must
be on its way. Earth is short, but Paradise is long
— there must be many moments in an eternal day;
then sometime we shall tarry while time and tide roll
on, and till then *vale*.

Your own dear

EMILIE.

[Written from Amherst between January 1, and the middle of
June, 1852.]

Sunday Evening.

MY VERY DEAR A., — I love to sit here alone,
writing a letter to you, and whether your joy in
reading will amount to as much or more, or even
less than mine in penning it to you, becomes to me
just now a very important problem — and I will
tax each power to solve the same for me; if as
happy, indeed, I have every occasion for gratitude
— more so, my absent friend, I may not hope to
make you, but I do hope most earnestly it may not
give you *less*. Oh, I do know it will not, if school-

day hearts are warm and school-day memories precious ! As I told you, it is Sunday to-day, so I find
myself quite curtailed in the selection of subjects,
being myself quite vain, and naturally adverting to
many worldly things which would doubtless grieve
and distress you : much more will I be restrained by
the fact that such stormy Sundays I always remain
at home, and have not those opportunities for hoard-
ing up great truths which I would have otherwise.
In view of these things, A., your kind heart will be
lenient, forgiving all empty words and unsatisfying
feelings on the Sabbath-day ground which we have
just alluded to. I rejoice in one theme appropriate
to every place and time — indeed it cannot intrude
in the hour most unseemly for every other thought
and every other feeling ; and sure I am to-day, how-
e'er it may be holy, I shall not break or reproach
by speaking of the links which bind us to each
other, and make the very thought of you, and time
when I last saw you, a sacred thing to me. And
I have many memories, and many thoughts beside,
which by some strange entwining, circle you round
and round ; if you please, a vine of fancies, towards
which dear A. sustains the part of oak, and as up
each sturdy branch there climbs a little tendril so
full of faith and confidence and the most holy trust,
so let the hearts do also, of the dear ' estray ; ' then
the farther we may be from home and from each
other, the nearer by that faith which ' overcometh
all things ' and bringeth us to itself.

Amherst and Philadelphia, separate indeed, and yet how near, bridged by a thousand trusts and a 'thousand times ten thousand' the travellers who cross, whom you and I may not see, nor hear the trip of their feet, yet faith tells us they are there, ever crossing and re-crossing. Very likely, A., you fancy me at home in my own little chamber, writing you a letter, but you are greatly mistaken. I am on the blue Susquehanna paddling down to you; I am not much of a sailor, so I get along rather slowly, and I am not much of a mermaid, though I verily think I shall be, if the tide overtakes me at my present jog. Hard-hearted girl! I don't believe you care, if you did you would come quickly and help me out of this sea; but if I drown, A., and go down to dwell in the seaweed forever and forever, I will not forget your name, nor all the wrong you did me!

Why did you go away and not come to see me? I felt so sure you would come, because you promised me, that I watched and waited for you, and bestowed a tear or two upon my absentee. How very sad it is to have a confiding nature, one's hopes and feelings are quite at the mercy of all who come along; and how very desirable to be a stolid individual, whose hopes and aspirations are safe in one's waistcoat pocket, and *that* a pocket indeed, and one not to be picked!

Notwithstanding your faithlessness I should have come to see you, but for that furious snow-storm;

I did attempt in spite of it, but it conquered in spite of me, and I doffed my hood and shawl, and felt very crestfallen the remainder of the day. I did want one more kiss, one sweet and sad good-by, before you had flown away; perhaps, my dear A., it is well that I go without it; it might have added anguish to our long separation, or made the miles still longer which keep a friend away. I always try to think in any disappointment that had I been gratified, it had been sadder still, and I weave from such supposition, *at times*, considerable consolation; consolation upside down as I am pleased to call it.

. . . Shall I have a letter soon — oh, may I very soon, for 'some days are dark and dreary, and the wind is never weary.'

EMILY E.

[Also written before the middle of June, 1852.]

Sabbath Day.

I love to link you, A. and E., I love to put you together and look at you side by side — the picture pleases me, and I should love to watch it until the sun goes down, did I not call to mind a very precious letter for which I have not as yet rendered a single farthing, so let me thank you that midst your many friends and cares and influenzas, you yet found time for me, and loved me. You remarked that I had written you more affectionately than wont — I have thought that word over and over, and it puzzles me now; whether our few last years have been cooler than our first ones, or whether I write

indifferently when I truly know it not, the query
troubles me.   I do believe sincerely, that the friendship formed at school was no warmer than now, nay
more, that *this* is warmest — they differ indeed to
me as morning differs from noon — one may be
fresher, cheerier, but the other fails not.

You and I have grown older since school-days,
and our years have made us soberer — I mean have
made *me* so, for you were always dignified, e'en
when a little girl, and *I* used, now and then, to
cut a timid caper.   That makes me think of you
the very first time I saw you, and I can't repress
a smile, not to say a hearty laugh, at your little
girl expense.   I have roused your curiosity, so I
will e'en tell you that one Wednesday afternoon,
in the days of that dear old Academy, I went in
to be entertained by the rhetoric of the gentlemen
and the milder form of the girls — I had hardly
recovered myself from the dismay attendant upon
entering august assemblies, when with the utmost
equanimity you ascended the stairs, bedecked with
dandelions, arranged, it seemed, for curls.   I shall
never forget that scene, if I live to have gray hairs,
nor the very remarkable fancies it gave me then of
you, and it comes over me now with the strangest
bygone funniness, and I laugh merrily.   Oh, A.,
you and the early flower are forever linked to me ;
as soon as the first green grass comes, up from a
chink in the stones peeps the little flower, precious
'leontodon,' and my heart fills toward you with a

warm and childlike fulness !   Nor do I laugh now ;
far from it, I rather bless the flower which sweetly,
slyly too, makes me come nearer you.

But, my dear, I can't give the dandelion the privilege due to you, so good-by, little one !

I would love to see you, A., I would rather than
write to you, might I with equal ease, for the
weather is very warm, and my head aches a little,
and my heart a little more, so taking me *collectively*,
I seem quite miserable, but I 'll give you the sunny
corners, and you must n't look at the shade.   You
were happy when you wrote me ; I hope so now,
though I would you were in the country, and could
reach the hills and fields.   I can reach them, carry
them home, which I do in my arms daily, and when
they drop and fade, I have only to gather fresh
ones.   Your joy would indeed be full, could you
sit as I, at my window, and hear the boundless birds,
and every little while feel the breath of some new
flower !   Oh, do you love the spring, and is n't it
brothers and sisters, and blessed, ministering spirits
unto you and me, and us all ?

I often see A. — oftener than at sometimes when
friendship drooped a little.   Did you ever know
that a flower, once withered and freshened again,
became an immortal flower, — that is, that it rises
again ?   I think resurrections here are sweeter, it
may be, than the longer and lasting one — for you
expect the one, and only hope for the other. . . .
I will show you the *sunset* if you will sit by me, but

I cannot bring it there, for so much gold is heavy. Can you see it in Philadelphia?

A rather long interval seems to have elapsed between the preceding letter and the next, which was written about July 26, probably of 1853. The hand-writing is quite different from the earlier letters, more resembling that middle period of which an illustration is given (page 218), yet still somewhat smaller.

The delicate and sunshiny sarcasm in this note may be the more fully appreciated by recalling that Emily Dickinson was not yet twenty-two years old.

Tuesday Evening.

MY DEAR CHILD, — Thank you for that sweet note which came so long ago, and thank you for asking me to come and visit you, and thank you for loving me, long ago, and to-day, and too for all the sweetness, and all the gentleness, and all the tenderness with which you remember me, — your quaint, old-fashioned friend.

I wanted very much to write you sooner, and I tried frequently, but till now in vain, and as I write to-night, it is with haste, and fear lest something still detain me. You know, my dear A., that the summer has been warm, that at this pleasant season we have much company, that this irresolute body refuses to serve sometimes, and the indignant tenant can only hold its peace, — all this you know, for I

have often told you, and yet I say it again, if mayhap it persuades you that I do love you indeed, and
have not done neglectfully. . . . I think it was in
June that your note reached here, and I did snatch
a moment to call upon˙ your friend.   Yet I went in
the dusk, and it was Saturday evening, so even then,
A., you see how cares pursued me.   I found her
very lovely in what she said to me, and I fancied in
her face so, although the gentle dusk would draw
her curtain close, and I did n't see her clearly.   We
talked the most of you, — a theme we surely loved,
or we had not discussed it in preference to all.   I
would love to meet her again, and give my love to
her, for your sake.   You asked me to come and see
you — I must speak of that.   I thank you, A., but
I don't go from home, unless emergency leads me
by the hand, and then I do it obstinately, and draw
back if I can.   Should I ever leave home, which is
improbable, I will, with much delight, accept your
invitation ; till then, my dear A., my warmest thanks
are yours, but don't expect me.   I 'm so old-fashioned, darling, that all your friends would stare.   I
should have to bring my work-bag, and my big
spectacles, and I half forgot my grandchildren, and
my pincushion, and puss — why, think of it seri-
ously, A., — do you think it my *duty* to leave ?   Will
you write me again ?   Mother and Vinnie send their
love, and here 's a kiss from me.

Good-night, from

EMILY.

CHAPTER II

To Mr William Austin Dickinson

THE following letters were written to
Emily Dickinson's brother between the
years 1847 and 1854, the earlier ones being
sent from South Hadley, while he was a student
in Amherst College. Later ones were written
at Amherst, and sent to Boston, where he had
charge of a school after graduation, 1851 and
1852; while the latest were addressed to Cambridge during her brother's studies at the
Harvard Law School, 1853 and 1854. During these last two years their father, the
Hon. Edward Dickinson, was in Congress at
Washington.

[South Hadley, Autumn, 1847.]

Thursday Noon.

MY DEAR BROTHER AUSTIN, — I have not really
a moment of time in which to write you, and am
taking time from ' silent study hours ; ' but I am
determined not to break my promise again, and I
generally carry my resolutions into effect. I watched
you until you were out of sight Saturday evening,

and then went to my room and looked over my treasures; and surely no miser ever counted his heaps of gold with more satisfaction than I gazed upon the presents from home. . . .

I can't tell you now how much good your visit did me. My spirits have wonderfully lightened since then. I had a great mind to be homesick after you went home, but I concluded not to, and therefore gave up all homesick feelings. Was not that a wise determination? . . .

There has been a menagerie here this week. Miss Lyon provided 'Daddy Hawks' as a beau for all the Seminary girls who wished to see the bears and monkeys, and your sister, not caring to go, was obliged to decline the gallantry of said gentleman, — which I fear I may never have another opportunity to avail myself of. The whole company stopped in front of the Seminary and played for about a quarter of an hour, for the purpose of getting custom in the afternoon, I opine. Almost all the girls went; and I enjoyed the solitude finely.

I want to know when you are coming to see me again, for I want to see you as much as I did before. I went to see Miss F. in her room yesterday. . . . I love her very much, and think I shall love all the teachers when I become better acquainted with them and find out their ways, which, I can assure you, are almost 'past finding out.'

I had almost forgotten to tell you of a dream

which I dreamed last night, and I would like to have you turn Daniel and interpret it to me ; or if you don't care about going through all the perils which he did, I will allow you to interpret it without, provided you will try to tell no lies about it. Well, I dreamed a dream, and lo ! father had failed, and mother said that 'our rye-field, which she and I planted, was mortgaged to Seth Nims.' I hope it is not true ; but do write soon and tell me, for you know I should expire of mortification to have our rye-field mortgaged, to say nothing of its falling into the merciless hands of a loco !

Won't you please to tell me when you answer my letter who the candidate for President is? I have been trying to find out ever since I came here, and have not yet succeeded. I don't know anything more about affairs in the world than if I were in a trance, and you must imagine with all your ' Sophomoric discernment ' that it is but little and very faint. Has the Mexican War terminated yet, and how? Are we beaten? Do you know of any nation about to besiege South Hadley? If so, do inform me of it, for I would be glad of a chance to escape, if we are to be stormed. I suppose Miss Lyon would furnish us all with daggers and order us to fight for our lives in case such perils should befall us. . . . Miss F. told me if I was writing to Amherst to send her love. Not specifying to whom, you may deal it out as your good sense and discretion prompt. Be a good boy and mind me !

[South Hadley, November 2, 1847.]

Tuesday Noon.

MY DEAR BROTHER AUSTIN, — I have this moment finished my recitation in history, and have a few minutes which I shall occupy in answering your short but welcome letter.   You probably heard that I was alive and well yesterday, unless Mr E. Dickinson was robbed of a note whose contents were to that effect.   But as robbers are not very plenty now-a-days, I will have no forebodings on that score, for the present.   How do you get along without me now, and does ' it seem any more like a funeral' than it did before your visit to your humble servant in this place?   Answer me !   I want much to see you all at home, and expect to three weeks from to-morrow if nothing unusual, like a famine or a pestilence, occurs to prevent my going home. I am anticipating much in seeing you on this week Saturday, and you had better not disappoint me ! for if you do, I will harness the ' furies,' and pursue you with ' a whip of scorpions,' which is even worse, you will find, than the ' long oat' which you may remember. . . . Tell father I am obliged to him much for his offers of pecuniary assistance, but do not need any.   We are furnished with an account-book here, and obliged to put down every mill which we spend, and what we spend it for, and show it to Miss Whitman every Saturday ; so you perceive your sister is learning accounts in

addition to the other branches of her education.
I am getting along nicely in my studies, and am
happy, quite, for me.

Do write a long letter to

Your affectionate sister,

EMILY.

Enclosed with this was a delicately written
'bill of fare' for one of the Seminary dinners.

SOUTH HADLEY SEMINARY

Nov. 2d, 1847

BILL OF FARE

ROAST VEAL
POTATOES
SQUASH
GRAVY
WHEAT AND BROWN BREAD
BUTTER
PEPPER AND SALT

Dessert

APPLE DUMPLING
SAUCE

WATER

Is n't that a dinner fit to set before a king?

[South Hadley, December 11, 1847.]

Saturday, P. M.

MY DEAR BROTHER AUSTIN, — . . . I finished my examination in Euclid last evening, and without a failure at any time. You can easily imagine how glad I am to get through with four books, for you have finished the whole forever. .. . . How are you all at home, and what are you doing this vacation? You are reading *Arabian Nights*, according to Viny's statement. I hope you have derived much benefit from their perusal, and presume your powers of imagining will vastly increase thereby. But I must give you a word of advice too. Cultivate your other powers in proportion as you allow imagination to captivate you. Am not I a very wise young lady?

I had almost forgotten to tell you what my studies are now — 'better late than never.' They are Chemistry, Physiology, and quarter course in Algebra. I have completed four studies already, and am getting along well. Did you think that it was my birthday yesterday? I don't believe I am *seventeen!* . . .

From your affectionate sister,

EMILY.

[South Hadley, about February 14, 1848.]

Thursday Morn.

MY DEAR AUSTIN, — You will perhaps imagine from my date that I am quite at leisure, and can do what I please even in the forenoon, but one of our teachers, who is engaged, received a visit from her intended quite unexpectedly yesterday afternoon, and she has gone to her home to show him, I opine, and will be absent until Saturday. As I happen to recite to her in one of my studies, her absence gives me a little time in which to write.

Your welcome letter found me all engrossed in the study of sulphuric acid! I deliberated for a few moments after its reception on the propriety of carrying it to Miss Whitman, your friend. The result of my deliberation was a conclusion to open it with moderation, peruse its contents with sobriety becoming my station, and if after a close investigation of its contents I found nothing which savored of rebellion or an unsubdued will, I would lay it away in my folio, and forget I had received it. Are you not gratified that I am so rapidly gaining correct ideas of female propriety and sedate deportment? After the proposed examination, finding it concealed no dangerous sentiments, I with great gravity deposited it with my other letters, and the impression that I once had such a letter is entirely obliterated by the waves of time.

I have been quite lonely since I came back, but cheered by the thought that I am not to return another year, I take comfort, and still hope on. My visit at home was happy, very happy to me; and had the idea of in so short a time returning been constantly in my dreams by night and day, I could not have been happier. 'There is no rose without a thorn' to me. Home was always dear to me, and dearer still the friends around it; but never did it seem so dear as now. All, all are kind to me, but their tones fall strangely on my ear, and their countenances meet mine not like home-faces, I can assure you most sincerely. Then when tempted to feel sad, I think of the blazing fire and the cheerful meal and the chair empty now I am gone. I can hear the cheerful voices and the merry laugh, and a desolate feeling comes home to my heart, to think I am alone. But my good angel only waits to see the tears coming and then whispers, 'Only this year! only twenty-two weeks more, and then home again you will be to stay.' To you, all busy and excited, I suppose the time flies faster; but to me slowly, very slowly, so that I can see his chariot wheels when they roll along, and himself is often visible. But I will no longer imagine, for your brain is full of *Arabian Nights'* fancies, and it will not do to pour fuel on your already kindled imagination. . . .

I suppose you have written a few and received a quantity of valentines this week. Every night have I looked, and yet in vain, for one of Cupid's messengers. Many of the girls have received very beautiful ones; and I have not quite done hoping for one. Surely my friend *Thomas* has not lost all his former affection for me! I entreat you to tell him I am pining for a valentine. I am sure I

shall not very soon forget last Valentine week, nor
any the sooner the fun I had at that time. . . .
Monday afternoon Mistress Lyon arose in the hall,
and forbade our sending 'any of those foolish notes
called valentines.' But those who were here last
year, knowing her opinions, were sufficiently cunning to write and give them into the care of D.
during the vacation; so that about 150 were de-
spatched on Valentine morn, before orders should
be put down to the contrary effect. Hearing of
this act, Miss Whitman, by and with the advice and
consent of the other teachers, with frowning brow,
sallied over to the Post Office to ascertain, if possible, the number of the valentines, and worse
still, the names of the offenders. Nothing has yet
been heard as to the amount of her information,
but as D. is a good hand to help the girls, and no
one has yet received sentence, we begin to think her
mission unsuccessful. I have not written one, nor
do I intend to.

Your injunction to pile on the wood has not been
unheeded, for we have been obliged to obey it to
keep from freezing up. . . . We cannot have much
more cold weather, I am sure, for spring is near.
. . . Professor Smith preached here last Sabbath,
and such sermons I never heard in my life. We
were all charmed with him, and dreaded to have
him close. . . .

Your affectionate sister,

EMILY.

[South Hadley, late May, 1848.]

Monday Morn.

MY DEAR AUSTIN,—I received a letter from home on Saturday by Mr G—— S——, and father wrote in it that he intended to send for cousin Emily and myself on Saturday of this week to spend the Sabbath at home. I went to Miss Whitman, after receiving the letter, and asked her if we could go if you decided to come for us. She seemed stunned by my request, and could not find utterance to an answer for some time. At length she said, ' Did you not know it was contrary to the rules of the Seminary to ask to be absent on the Sabbath?' I told her I did not. She then took a Catalogue from her table, and showed me the law in full at the last part of it. She closed by saying that we could not go, and I returned to my room without farther ado. So you see I shall be deprived of the pleasure of a visit home, and you that of seeing me, if I may have the presumption to call it a pleasure ! The teachers are not willing to let the girls go home this term as it is the last one, and as I have only nine weeks more to spend here, we had better be contented to obey the commands. We shall only be the more glad to see one another after a longer absence, that will be all. I was highly edified with your imaginative note to me, and think your flights of fancy indeed wonderful at your age ! When are you coming to see me — it would be very pleasant to us to receive a visit from your highness

if you can be absent from home long enough for such
a purpose. . . . I can't write longer.
                    Your affectionate sister,
                                                EMILIE.

The next letter was written three years later,
and sent to Boston.

                    [Amherst, early in 1851.]
                                        Sunday Evening.

It might not come amiss, dear Austin, to have a tiding or two concerning our state and feelings, particularly when we remember that 'Jamie has gone awa'.'

Our state is pretty comfortable, and our feelings
are somewhat solemn, which we account for satis-
factorily by calling to mind the fact that it is the
Sabbath day. Whether a certain passenger in a certain yesterday's stage has any sombre effect on our
once merry household or the reverse, 'I dinna choose
to tell,' but be the case as it may, we are rather a
crestfallen company, to make the best of us, and
what with the sighing wind, the sobbing rain, and
the whining of Nature generally, we can hardly contain ourselves, and I only hope and trust that your
this-evening's-lot is cast in far more cheery places
than the ones you leave behind.

We are enjoying this evening what is called a
'northeast storm' — a little north of east in case
you are pretty definite. Father thinks it's 'amazin'
raw,' and I'm half disposed to think that he's in the
right about it, though I keep pretty dark and don't

say much about it! Vinnie is at the instrument, humming a pensive air concerning a young lady who thought she was 'almost there.' Vinnie seems much grieved, and I really suppose *I* ought to betake myself to weeping; I 'm pretty sure that I *shall* if she don't abate her singing.

Father 's just got home from meeting and Mr Boltwood's, found the last quite comfortable and the first not quite so well. . . . There has been not much stirring since when you went away — I should venture to say prudently that matters had come to a stand — unless something new 'turns up,' I cannot see anything to prevent a quiet season. Father takes care of the doors and mother of the windows, and Vinnie and I are secure against all outward attacks. If we can get our hearts 'under,' I don't have much to fear — I 've got all but three feelings down, if I can only keep them! . . .

I shall think of you to-morrow with four and twenty Irish boys all in a row. I miss you very much — I put on my bonnet to-night, opened the gate very desperately, and for a little while the suspense was terrible — I think I was held in check by some invisible agent, for I returned to the house without having done any harm!

If I had n't been afraid that you would 'poke fun' at my feelings, I had written a sincere letter, but since 'the world is hollow, and dollie 's stuffed with sawdust,' I really do not think we had better expose our feelings. . . .

Your dear sister,   EMILY.

[Amherst, 1851.]

Sunday Evening.

I received your letter, Austin, permit me to thank you for it and to request some more as soon as it's convenient — permit me to accord with your discreet opinion concerning Swedish Jennie, and to commend the heart brave enough to express it — combating the opinion of two civilized worlds and New York into the bargain must need considerable daring — indeed, it had never occurred to me that amidst the hallelujahs one tongue would dare be dumb, and much less, I assure you, that this dissenting one should be my romantic brother ! For I had looked for delight and a very high style of rapture in such a youth as you. . . .

We have all been rather piqued at Jennie's singing so well, and this first calumnious whisper pleases us so well, we rejoice that we did n't come — our visit is yet before us. . . . You have n't told us yet as you promised about your home — what kind of people they are — whether you find them pleasant — whether those timid gentlemen have yet 'found tongues to say.' Do you find the life and living any more annoying than you at first expected — do you light upon any friends to help the time away — have you whipped any more bad boys — all these are solemn questions, pray give them proper heed !

Two weeks of your time are gone ; I can't help wondering sometimes if you would love to see us,

and come to this still home. . . . A Senior levee
was held at Professor and Mrs Haven's on Tuesday
of last week — Vinnie played pretty well.   There's
another at the President's this next Friday evening.
Clarum et venerabile Seniors !

[Amherst, March, 1851.]

Sunday Afternoon.

. . . It's a glorious afternoon — the sky is blue
and warm — the wind blows just enough to keep the
clouds sailing, and the sunshine — oh *such* sunshine !
It is n't like gold, for gold is dim beside it ; it is n't
like anything which you or I have seen !   It seems
to me 'Ik Marvel' was born on such a day ; I only
wish you were here.   Such days were made on purpose for you and me ; then what in the world are
you gone for?   Oh, dear, I do not know, but this I
do know, that if wishing would bring you home, you
were here to-day.   Is it pleasant in Boston?   *Of
course* it is n't, though.   I might have known more
than to make such an inquiry.   No doubt the streets
are muddy, and the sky some dingy hue, and I can
think just how everything bangs and rattles, and
goes rumbling along through stones and plank and
clay !   I don't feel as if I could have you there, possibly, another day.   I 'm afraid you 'll turn into a
bank, or a Pearl Street counting-room, if you have
not already assumed some monstrous shape, living
in such a place.

Let me see — April ; three weeks until April —

the very first of April — well, perhaps that will do,
only be sure of the week, the *whole* week, and nothing but the week.   If they make new arrangements,
give my respects to them, and tell them old arrangements are good enough for you, and you will have
them ; then if they raise the wind, why, let it blow
— there 's nothing more excellent than a breeze
now and then !

What a time we shall have Fast day, after we get
home from meeting — why, it makes me dance to
think of it ; and Austin, if I dance so many days
beforehand, what will become of me when the hour
really arrives?   I don't know, I 'm sure ; and I don't
care, much, for that or for anything else but get you
home. . . . Much love from mother and Vinnie ;
we are now pretty well, and our hearts are set on
April, the *very first* of April !

EMILIE.

[Amherst, late March, 1851.]
Thursday Night.

DEAR AUSTIN, — . . . I have read *Ellen Middle-
ton*.   I need n't tell you I like it, nor need I tell
you more, for you know already.

I thank you more and more for all the pleasures
you give me — I can give you nothing, Austin, but
a warm and grateful heart that is yours now and
always.   Love from all.

EMILIE.

Only think, you are coming Saturday !   I don't

know why it is that it's always *Sunday* immediately you get home. I will arrange it differently. If it was n't twelve o'clock I would stay longer.

[Amherst, June 16, 1851.]

Sunday Evening.

. . . I'm glad you are so well pleased, I'm glad you are *not* delighted. I would not that foreign places should wear the smile of home. We are quite alarmed for the *boys* — hope you won't kill or pack away any of 'em — so near Dr Webster's bones 't is not strange you have had temptations ! . . . The country's still just now, and the severities alluded to will have a salutary influence in waking the people up.   Speaking of *getting up*, how early are metropolitans expected to wake up, especially young men — more especially school-masters?   I miss my 'department' mornings.   I lay it quite to heart that I've no one to wake up. *Your* room looks lonely enough, I do not love to go in there ; whenever I pass through I find I 'gin to whistle, as we read that little boys are wont to do in the graveyard.   I am going to set out crickets as soon as I find time, that they by their shrill singing shall help disperse the gloom ; will they grow if I transplant them?

You importune me for news ; I am very sorry to say 'Vanity of vanities' there 's no such thing as news — it is almost time for the cholera, and then things will take a start ! . . . All of the folks send love.

Your affectionate

EMILY.

[July 5, 1851.]

Sunday Afternoon.

I have just come in from church very hot and faded. . . . Our church grows interesting — Zion lifts her head — I overhear remarks signifying Jerusalem, — I do not feel at liberty to say any more to-day !

. . . I wanted to write you Friday, the night of Jennie Lind, but reaching home past midnight, and my room sometime after, encountering several perils starting and on the way, among which a kicking horse, an inexperienced driver, a number of Jove's thunderbolts, and a very terrible rain, are worthy to have record. All of us went — just four — add an absent individual and that will make full five. The concert commenced at eight, but knowing the world was *hollow* we thought we 'd start at six, and come up with everybody that meant to come up with us ; we had proceeded some steps when one of the beasts showed symptoms ; and just by the blacksmith's shop exercises commenced, consisting of kicking and plunging on the part of the horse, and whips and moral suasion from the gentleman who drove — the horse refused to proceed, and your respected family with much chagrin dismounted, advanced to the hotel, and for a season halted ; another horse procured, we were politely invited to take our seats, and proceed, which we refused to do till the animal was warranted. About half through our journey thunder was said to be heard, and a suspicious cloud came travelling up the sky. What words express our horror when rain began to fall, in drops, sheets, cataracts — what fancy conceive of drippings and of drenchings which we met on the way; how the stage and its mourning captives drew up at Warner's Hotel; how all of us alighted, and were conducted in, — how the rain did not abate, — how we walked in silence to the old Edwards church[1] and took our seats in the same — how Jennie came out like a child and sang and sang again — how bouquets fell in showers, and the roof was rent with applause — how it thundered outside, and inside with the thunder of God and of men — judge ye which was the loudest; how we all loved Jennie Lind, but not accustomed oft to her manner of singing did n't fancy *that* so well as we did *her*. No doubt it was very fine, but take some notes from her *Echo*, the bird sounds from the *Bird Song*, and some of her curious trills, and I 'd rather have a Yankee.

Herself and not her music was what we seemed to love — she has an air of exile in her mild blue eyes, and a something sweet and touching in her native accent which charms her many friends. *Give me my thatched cottage* as she sang she grew so earnest she seemed half lost in song, and for a transient time I fancied she *had* found it and would be

[1] Evidently a slip of the pen, as Jenny Lind sang in the old First Church at Northampton on that occasion.

seen 'na mair;' and then her foreign accent made her again a wanderer — we will talk about her sometime when you come. Father sat all the evening looking *mad*, and yet so much amused you would have *died* a-laughing. . . . It was n't sarcasm exactly, nor it was n't disdain, it was infinitely funnier than either of those virtues, as if old Abraham had come to see the show, and thought it was all very well, but a little excess of *monkey!* She took $4,000 for tickets at Northampton aside from all expenses. . . .

About our coming to Boston — we think we shall probably come — we want to see our friends, yourself and Aunt L.'s family. We don't care a fig for the Museum, the stillness, or Jennie Lind. . . . Love from us all.

Your affectionate sister,

EMILY.

[Late July, 1851.]

Sunday Evening.

. . . Oh how I wish I could see your world and its little kingdoms, and I wish I could see the king — Stranger! he was my brother! I fancy little boys of several little sizes, some of them clothed in blue cloth, some of them clad in gray — I seat them round on benches in the school-room of my mind — then I set them all to shaking — on peril of their lives that they move their lips or whisper; then I clothe you with authority and empower you to punish, and to enforce the law, I call you 'Rabbi, Master,' and the picture is complete!   It would seem very funny, say for Vinnie and me to come round as Committee — we should enjoy the terrors of fifty little boys, and any specimens of discipline in your way would be a rare treat for us.   I should love to know how you managed — whether government as a science is laid down and executed, or whether you *cuff* and *thrash* as the occasion dictates; whether you use *pure* law as in the case of commanding, or whether you enforce it by means of sticks and stones as in the case of agents.   I suppose you have authority bounded but by their lives. . . . I should think you'd be tired of school and teaching and such hot weather.   I really wish you were here, and the Endicott school where you found it.   Whenever we go to ride in our beautiful family carriage we think if 'wishes were horses' we four 'beggars would ride.'   We shall enjoy brimful everything now but half full, and to have you home once more will be like living again.

We are having a pleasant summer — without one of the five it is yet a lonely one.   Vinnie says sometimes — Did n't we have a brother — it seems to me we did, his name was Austin — we call but he answers not again — echo, Where is Austin? laughing, 'Where *is* Austin?' . . . I wish they need not exhibit just for once in the year, and give you up on Saturday instead of the next week Wednesday; but keep your courage up and show forth those

Emerald Isles till school committees and mayors are blinded with the dazzling! Would n't I love to be there! . . .

Our apples are ripening fast. I am fully convinced that with your approbation they will not only pick themselves, but arrange one another in baskets and present themselves to be eaten.

Love from all.

EMILIE.

[August, 1851.]

Sunday Afternoon.

At my old stand again, dear Austin, and happy as a queen to know that while I speak those whom I love are listening, and I am happier still if I shall make them happy.

I have just finished reading your letter which was brought in since church. I like it grandly — very — because it is so long, and also it's *so* funny — we have all been laughing till the old house rung again at your delineation of men, women, and things. I feel quite like retiring in presence of one so grand, and casting my small lot among small birds and fishes; you say you don't comprehend me, you want a simpler style — gratitude indeed for all my fine philosophy! I strove to be exalted, thinking I might reach *you*, and while I pant and struggle and climb the nearest cloud, you walk out very leisurely in your slippers from Empyrean, and without the slightest notice, request me to get down! As simple as you please, the simplest sort of simple — I 'll

be a little ninny, a little pussy catty, a little Red
Riding Hood; I'll wear a bee in my bonnet, and
a rose-bud in my hair, and what remains to do
you shall be told hereafter.

Your letters are richest treats, send them always
just such warm days — they are worth a score of
fans and many refrigerators — the only difficulty
they are so *queer*, and laughing such hot weather is
anything but amusing. A little more of earnest,
and a little less of jest until we are out of August,
and then you may joke as freely as the father of
rogues himself, and we will banish care, and daily
die a-laughing !

It is very hot here now; I don't believe it's any
hotter in Boston than it is here. . . . Vinnie suggests
that she may sometimes occur to mind when you
would like more collars made. I told her I wouldn't
tell you — I haven't, however, decided whether I
will or not.

I often put on five knives and forks, and another
tumbler, forgetting for the moment that 'we are
not all here.' It occurs to me, however, and I
remove the extra, and brush a tear away in memory
of my brother.

We miss you now and always. When God bestows but three, and one of those is withdrawn,
the others are left alone. . . . Father is as uneasy
when you are gone away as if you catch a trout
and put him in Sahara. When you first went away
he came home very frequently — walked gravely

towards the barn, and returned looking very stately
— then strode away down street as if the foe was
coming; *now* he is more resigned — contents himself by fancying that 'we shall hear to-day,' and
then when we do not hear, he wags his head profound, and thinks without a doubt there will be
news 'to-morrow.' 'Once one is two,' once one will
be two — ah, I have it here!

I wish you could have some cherries — if there
was any way we would send you a basket of them —
they are very large and delicious, and are just ripening now. Little Austin Grout comes every day to
pick them, and mother takes great comfort in calling him by name, from vague association with her
departed boy. Austin, to tell the truth, it is very
still and lonely — I do wish you were here. . . .
The railroad is 'a-workin'.' My love to all my
friends. I am on my way downstairs to put the
tea-kettle boiling — writing and taking tea cannot
sympathize. If you forget me now, your right hand
shall its cunning.

EMILIE.

[Written after a visit of the sisters in Boston. Amherst,
September 24, 1851.]

Tuesday Evening.

We have got home, dear Austin. It is very lonely
here — I have tried to make up my mind which was
better, home and parents and country, or city and
smoke and dust shared with the only being whom I

can call my brother. The scales *don't* poise very evenly, but so far as I can judge, the balance is in your favor. The folks are much more lonely than while we were away — they say they seemed to feel that we were straying together and together would return, and the unattended sisters seemed very sad to them. . . . They have had a number of friends to call and visit with them. Mother never was busier than while we were away — what with fruit and plants and chickens and sympathizing friends she really was so hurried she hardly knew what to do.

Vinnie and I came safely, and met with no mishap — the bouquet was not withered nor was the bottle cracked. It was fortunate for the freight car that Vinnie and I were there, ours being the only baggage passing along the line. The folks looked very funny who travelled with us that day — they were dim and faded, like folks passed away — the conductor seemed so grand with about half a dozen tickets which he dispersed and demanded in a very small space of time — I judged that the minority were travelling that day, and could n't hardly help smiling at our ticket friend, however sorry I was at the small amount of people passing along his way. He looked as if he wanted to make an apology for not having more travellers to keep him company.

The route and the cars seemed strangely — there were no boys with fruit, there were no boys with pamphlets; one fearful little fellow ventured into the car with what appeared to be publications and tracts; he offered them to no one, and no one inquired for them, and he seemed greatly relieved that no one wanted to buy them. . . . Mother sends much love, and Vinnie.

Your lonely sister,

EMILY.

[Amherst, Autumn, 1851.]

Saturday Morn.

DEAR AUSTIN, — I've been trying to think this morning how many weeks it was since you went away — I fail in calculations; it seems so long to me since you went back to school that I set down days for years, and weeks for a score of years — not reckoning time by minutes, I don't know what to think of such great discrepancies between the actual hours and those which 'seem to be.' It may seem long to you since you returned to Boston — how I wish you would stay and never go back again. Everything is so still here, and the clouds are cold and gray — I think it will rain soon. Oh, I am so lonely! . . . You had a windy evening going back to Boston, and we thought of you many times and hoped you would not be cold. Our fire burned so cheerfully I couldn't help thinking of how many were here, and how many were away, and I wished so many times during that long evening that the door would open and you come walking in. Home is a holy thing, — nothing of doubt or distrust can enter its blessed portals. I feel it more and more as the great world goes on, and one and another forsake in whom you place your trust, here seems indeed to be a bit of Eden which not the sin of any can utterly destroy, — smaller it is indeed, and it may be less fair, but fairer it is and brighter than all the world beside.

I hope this year in Boston will not impair your health, and I hope you will be as happy as you used to be before. I don't wonder it makes you sober to leave this blessed air — if it were in my power I would on every morning transmit its purest breaths fragrant and cool to you. How I wish you could have it — a thousand little winds waft it to me this morning, fragrant with forest leaves and bright autumnal berries. I would be willing to give you my portion for to-day, and take the salt sea's breath in its bright, bounding stead. . . .

Your affectionate

EMILY.

. . . Mother sends her love and your waistcoat, thinking you 'll like the one, and quite likely need the other.

[Amherst, October 2, 1851.]

Wednesday Noon.

We are just through dinner, Austin, I want to write so much that I omit digestion, and a dyspepsia will probably be the result. . . . I received your letter yesterday. . . . You say we must n't trouble to send you any fruit, also your clothes must give us no uneasiness. I don't ever want to have you say any more such things. They make me feel like crying. If you 'd only teased us for it, and declared that you would have it, I should n't have cared so much that we could find no way to send you any, but you resign so cheerfully your birthright of purple grapes, and do not so much as murmur at the departing peaches, that I hardly can taste the one or drink the juice of the other. They are so beautiful, Austin, — we have such an abundance 'while you perish with hunger.'

I do hope some one will make up a mind to go before our peaches are quite gone. The world is full of people travelling everywhere, until it occurs to you that you will send an errand, and then by 'hook or crook' you can't find any traveller who, for money or love, can be induced to go and carry the opprobrious package. It 's a very selfish age, that is all I can say about it. Mr Storekeeper S—— has been 'almost persuaded' to go, but I believe he has put it off 'till a more convenient season,' so to show my disapprobation I sha'n't buy any more gloves at Mr S——'s store! Don't you think it will seem very cutting to see me pass by his goods and purchase at Mr K——'s? I don't think I shall retract should he regret his course and decide to go to-morrow, because it is the principle of disappointing people which I disapprove! . . .

The peaches are very large — one side a rosy cheek, and the other a golden, and that peculiar coat of velvet and of down which makes a peach so beautiful. The grapes, too, are fine, juicy, and *such* a purple — I fancy the robes of kings are not a tint more royal. The vine looks like a kingdom, with ripe round grapes for kings, and hungry mouths for subjects — the first instance on record of subjects devouring kings ! You *shall* have some grapes, dear Austin, if I have to come on foot in order to bring them to you.

The apples are very fine — it is n't quite time to pick them — the cider is almost done — we shall have some I guess by Saturday, at any rate Sunday noon. The vegetables are not gathered, but will be before very long. The horse is doing nicely ; he travels ' like a bird ' to use a favorite phrase of your delighted mother's. You ask about the leaves — shall I say they are falling ? They had begun to fall before Vinnie and I came home, and we walked up the steps through little brown ones rustling. . . .

Vinnie tells me she has detailed the news — she reserved the deaths for me, thinking I might fall short of my usual letter somewhere. In accordance with her wishes I acquaint you with the decease of your aged friend Deacon ——. He had no disease that we know of, but gradually went out. . . . Monday evening we were all startled by a violent church-bell ringing, and thinking of nothing but fire, rushed out in the street to see. The sky was a beautiful red, bordering on a crimson, and rays of a gold pink color were constantly shooting off from a kind of sun in the centre. People were alarmed at this beautiful phenomenon, supposing that fires somewhere were coloring the sky. The exhibition lasted for nearly fifteen minutes, and the streets were full of people wondering and admiring. Father happened to see it among the very first, and rang the bell himself to call attention to it. You will have a full account from the pen of Mr Trumbull, who, I have not a doubt, was seen with a long lead pencil a-noting down the sky at the time of its highest glory. . . . You will be here now so soon — we are impatient for it — we want to see you, Austin, how much I cannot say here.

Your affectionate

EMILY.

[Amherst, early October, 1851.]

Friday Morning.

DEAR AUSTIN, — . . . I would not spend much strength upon those little school-boys — you will need it all for something better and braver after you get away. It would rejoice my heart if on some pleasant morning you'd turn the school-room key on Irish boys, nurse and all, and walk away to freedom and the sunshine here at home. Father says all Boston wouldn't be a temptation to you another year — I wish it would not tempt you to stay another day. Oh, Austin, it is wrong to tantalize you so while

you are braving all things in trying to fulfil duty.
Duty is black and brown — home is bright and shin-
ing, 'and the spirit and the bride say come, and let
him that' wandereth come, for 'behold all things
are ready.' We are having such lovely weather —
the air is as sweet and still — now and then a gay
leaf falling — the crickets sing all day long — high
in a crimson tree a belated bird is singing — a
thousand little painters are tingeing hill and dale. I
admit now, Austin, that autumn is *most* beautiful,
and spring is but the least, yet they ' differ as
stars' in their distinctive glories. How happy if you
were here to share these pleasures with us — the
fruit should be more sweet, and the dying day more
golden — merrier the falling nut if with you we
gathered it and hid it down deep in the abyss of
basket ; but you complain not, wherefore do we ?

Tuesday evening we had a beautiful time reading
and talking of the good times of last summer, and
we anticipated — boasted ourselves of to-morrow —
of the future we created, and all of us went to ride
in an air-bubble for a carriage. We cherish all the
past, we glide a-down the present, awake yet dreaming ; but the future of ours together — there the bird
sings loudest, and the sun shines always there. . . .

I had a dissertation from E. C. a day or two ago
— don't know which was the author, Plato or Socrates — rather think Jove had a finger in it. . . .
They all send their love. Vinnie sends hers. How
soon you will be here ! Days, flee away — 'lest with

a whip of scorpions I overtake your lingering.' I am
in a hurry — this pen is too slow for me — 'it hath
done what it could.'

Your affectionate

EMILY.

[Amherst, before ' Cattle Show,' 1851.]

Friday Morning.

. . . The breakfast is so warm, and pussy is here
a-singing, and the tea-kettle sings too, as if to see
which was loudest, and I am so afraid lest kitty
should be beaten — yet a shadow falls upon my
morning picture — where is the youth so bold, the
bravest of our fold — a seat is empty here —
spectres sit in your chair, and now and then nudge
father with their long, bony elbows. I wish you were
here, dear Austin; the dust falls on the bureau in
your deserted room, and gay, frivolous spiders spin
away in the corners. I don't go there after dark
whenever I can help it, for the twilight seems to
pause there, and I am half afraid; and if ever I have
to go, I hurry with all my might, and never look behind me, for I know who I should see.

Before next Tuesday — oh, before the coming
stage, will I not brighten and brush it, and open
the long-closed blinds, and with a sweeping broom
will I not bring each spider down from its home
so high, and tell it it may come back again when
master has gone — and oh, I will bid it to be a
tardy spider, to tarry on the way; and I will think

my eye is fuller than sometimes, though *why* I cannot tell, when it shall rap on the window and come to live again. I am so happy when I know how soon you are coming that I put away my sewing and go out in the yard to think. I have tried to delay the frosts, I have coaxed the fading flowers, I thought I *could* detain a few of the crimson leaves until you had smiled upon them; but their companions call them, and they cannot stay away.

You will find the blue hills, Austin, with the autumnal shadows silently sleeping on them, and there will be a glory lingering round the day, so you'll know autumn has been here; and the setting sun will tell you, if you don't get home till evening. . . . I thank you for such a long letter, and yet if I might choose, the next should be a longer. I think a letter just about three days long would make me happier than any other kind of one, if you please, — dated at Boston, but thanks be to our Father you may conclude it here. Everything has changed since my other letter, — the doors are shut this morning, and all the kitchen wall is covered with chilly flies who are trying to warm themselves, — poor things, they do not understand that there are no summer mornings remaining to them and me, and they have a bewildered air which is really very droll, did n't one feel sorry for them. You would say 't was a gloomy morning if you were sitting here, — the frost has been severe, and the few lingering leaves seem anxious to be going, and wrap their

faded cloaks more closely about them as if to shield
them from the chilly northeast wind. The earth
looks like some poor old lady who by dint of pains
has bloomed e'en till now, yet in a forgetful moment a few silver hairs from out her cap come
stealing, and she tucks them back so hastily and
thinks nobody sees. The cows are going to pasture,
and little boys with their hands in their pockets are
whistling to try to keep warm. Don't think that the
sky will frown so the day when you come home!
She will smile and look happy, and be full of sunshine then, and even should she frown upon her
child returning, there is another sky, ever serene
and fair, and there is another sunshine, though it be
darkness there; never mind faded forests, Austin,
never mind silent fields — *here* is a little forest,
whose leaf is ever green; here is a brighter garden,
where not a frost has been; in its unfading flowers I
hear the bright bee hum; prithee, my brother, into
my garden come!

      Your very affectionate sister.

[November, 1851.]

Thursday Evening.

DEAR AUSTIN, — Something seems to whisper
'He is thinking of home this evening,' perhaps
because it rains, perhaps because it's evening and
the orchestra of winds perform their strange, sad
music. I wouldn't wonder if home were thinking

of him ; and it seems so natural for one to think of
the other, perhaps it is no superstition or omen of
this evening, — no omen ' at all, at all,' as Mrs
Mack would say.

Father is staying at home this evening it is so
inclement — Vinnie diverts his mind with little
snatches of music ; and mother mends a garment
to make it snugger for you — and what do you
think *I* do among this family circle? I am thinking of you with all my might, and it just occurs to
me to note a few of my thoughts for your own inspec-
tion. 'Keeping a diary' is not familiar to me as
to your sister Vinnie, but her own bright example
is quite a comfort to me, so I 'll try.

I waked up this morning thinking for all the
world I had had a letter from you — just as the
seal was breaking, father rapped at my door. I
was sadly disappointed not to go on and read ; but
when the four black horses came trotting into town,
and their load was none the heavier by a tiding
for me — I was not disappointed then, it was harder
to me than had I been disappointed. . . . I found
I had made no provision for any such time as that.
. . . The weather has been unpleasant ever since
you went away — Monday morning we waked up
in the midst of a furious snow-storm — the snow
was the depth of an inch ; oh, it looked so wintry !
By-and-by the sun came out, but the wind blew
violently and it grew so cold that we gathered all
the quinces, put up the stove in the sitting-room,

and bade the world good-by. Kind clouds came
over at evening ; still the sinking thermometer gave
terrible signs of what would be on the morning.
At last the morning came, laden with mild south
winds, and the winds have brought the rain, so
here we are. . . . Your very hasty letter just at
your return rejoiced us — that you were ' better —
happier — heartier.' What made you think of such
beautiful words to tell us how you were, and how
cheerful you were feeling? It did us a world of
good. How little the scribe thinks of the value of
his line — how many eager eyes will search its every
meaning, how much swifter the strokes of ' the
little mystic clock, no human eye hath seen, which
ticketh on and ticketh on, from morning until e'en.'
If it were not that I could write you, you could not go
away ; therefore pen and ink are very excellent things.

We had new brown bread for tea — when it came
smoking on and we sat around the table, how I did
wish a slice could be reserved for you ! You shall
have as many loaves as we have eaten slices if you
will but come home. This suggests Thanksgiving,
you will soon be here ; then I can't help thinking
of how, when we rejoice, so many hearts are breaking next Thanksgiving day. What will you say,
Austin, if I tell you that Jennie Grout and merry
Martha Kingman will spend the day above? They
are not here — ' While we delayed to let them
forth, angels beyond stayed for them.' . . .

Your affectionate

EMILY.

[Amherst, November 17, 1851.]

Sunday Afternoon.

DEAR AUSTIN, — We have just got home from
meeting — it is very windy and cold — the hills
from our kitchen window are just crusted with snow,
which with their blue mantillas makes them seem so
beautiful.   You sat just here last Sunday, where I
am sitting now ; and our voices were nimbler than
our pens can be, if they try never so hardly.   I
should be quite sad to-day, thinking about last Sunday, did n't another Sabbath smile at me so pleasantly,
promising me on its word to present you here
again when ' six days' work is done.'

Father and mother sit in state in the sitting-
room perusing such papers, only, as they are well
assured, have nothing carnal in them ; Vinnie is
eating an apple which makes me think of gold,
and accompanying it with her favorite *Observer*,
which, if you recollect, deprives us many a time of
her sisterly society.   Pussy has n't returned from
the afternoon assembly, so you have us all just
as we are at present.   We were very glad indeed
to hear from you so soon, glad that a cheerful fire
met you at the door.   I *do* well remember how
chilly the west wind blew, and how everything
shook and rattled before I went to sleep, and I
often thought of you in the midnight car, and hoped
you were not lonely. . . . We are thinking most of
Thanksgiving than anything else just now — how

full will be the circle, less then by none — how the things will smoke — how the board will groan with the thousand savory viands — how when the day is done, lo, the evening cometh, laden with merrie laugh and happy conversation, and then the sleep and the dream each of a knight or ' Ladie '— how I love to see them, a beautiful company coming down the hill which men call the Future, with their hearts full of joy and their hands of gladness. Thanksgiving indeed to a family united once more together before they go away. . . . Don't mind the days — some of them are long ones, but who cares for length when breadth is in store for him? Or who minds the cross who knows he'll have a crown? I wish I could imbue you with all the strength and courage which can be given men — I wish I could assure you of the constant remembrance of those you leave at home — I wish — but oh ! how vainly — that I could bring you back again and never more to stray. You are tired now, dear Austin, with my incessant din, but I can't help saying any of these things.

The very warmest love from Vinnie and every one of us. I am never ready to go.

Reluctant

EMILY.

[December, 1851].

Monday Morning.

DEAR AUSTIN, — . . . I was so glad to get your letter. I had been making calls all Saturday afternoon, and came home very tired, and a little disconsolate, so your letter was more than welcome. . . . Oh Austin, you don't know how we all wished for you yesterday. We had such a splendid sermon from Professor Park — I never heard anything like it, and don't expect to again, till we stand at the great white throne, and 'he reads from the Book, the Lamb's Book.' The students and chapel people all came to our church, and it was very full, and still, so still the buzzing of a fly would have boomed like a cannon. And when it was all over, and that wonderful man sat down, people stared at each other, and looked as wan and wild as if they had seen a spirit, and wondered they had not died. How I wish you had heard him — I thought of it all the time. . . .

Affectionately,

EMILIE.

[Amherst, January, 1852.]

Monday Morning.'

Did you think I was tardy, Austin? For two Sunday afternoons it has been so cold and cloudy that I did n't feel in my very happiest mood, and so I did not write until next Monday morning, determin-

ing in my heart never to write to you in any but
cheerful spirits.

Even this morning, Austin, I am not in merry
case, for it snows slowly and solemnly, and hardly
an outdoor thing can be seen a-stirring — now and
then a man goes by with a large cloak wrapped
around him, and shivering at that; and now and
then a stray kitten out on some urgent errand creeps
through the flakes and crawls so fast as *may* crawl
half frozen away. I am glad for the sake of your
body that you are not here this morning, for it is a
trying time for fingers and toes — for the heart's
sake I would verily have you here. You know there
are winter mornings when the cold without only
adds to the warm within, and the more it snows and
the harder it blows brighter the fires blaze, and
chirps more merrily the 'cricket on the hearth.'
It is hardly cheery enough for such a scene this
morning, and yet methinks it would be if you were
only here. The future full of sleigh-rides would
chase the gloom from our minds which only deepens
and darkens with every flake that falls.

Black Fanny would 'toe the mark' if you should
be here to-morrow; but as the prospects are, I presume Black Fanny's hoofs will not attempt to fly.
Do you have any snow in Boston? Enough for a
ride, I hope, for the sake of 'Auld Lang Syne.'
Perhaps the 'ladie' of curls would not object to a
drive. . . . We miss you more and more, we do
not become accustomed to separation from you.

I almost wish sometimes we need n't miss you so
much, since duty claims a year of you entirely to
herself; and then again I think that it is pleasant to
miss you if you must go away, and I would not have
it otherwise, even if I could.   In every pleasure and
pain you come up to our minds so wishfully — we
know you 'd enjoy our joy, and if you were with us,
Austin, we could bear little trials more cheerfully.
. . . When I know of anything funny I am just as apt
to cry, far more so than to laugh, for I know who
loves jokes best, and who is not here to enjoy them.
We don't have many jokes, though, now, it is pretty
much all sobriety; and we do not have much poetry,
father having made up his mind that it 's pretty
much all real life.   Father's real life and mine
sometimes come into collision but as yet escape un-
hurt. . . .   I am so glad you are well and in such
happy spirits — both happy and well is a great comfort to us when you are far away.

Emilie.

[February 6, 1852.]

Friday Morning.

. . . Since we have written you the grand railroad decision is made, and there is great rejoicing
throughout this town and the neighboring; that
is, Sunderland, Montague, and Belchertown. Everybody is wide awake, everything is stirring, the streets
are full of people walking cheeringly, and you should
really be here to partake of the jubilee.   The event

was celebrated by D. Warner and cannon; and the silent satisfaction in the hearts of all is its crowning attestation.

Father is really sober from excessive satisfaction, and bears his honors with a most becoming air. Nobody believes it yet, it seems like a fairy tale, a most miraculous event in the lives of us all. The men begin working next week; only think of it, Austin; why, I verily believe we shall fall down and worship the first 'son of Erin' that comes, and the first sod he turns will be preserved as an emblem of the struggle and victory of our heroic fathers. Such old fellows as Col. S. and his wife fold their arms complacently and say, 'Well, I declare, we have got it after all.' Got it, *you* good-for-nothings! and so we have, in spite of sneers and pities and insults from all around; and we will keep it too, in spite of earth and heaven! How I wish you were here — it is really too bad, Austin, at such a time as now. I miss your big hurrahs, and the famous stir you make upon all such occasions; but it is a comfort to know that you are here — that your whole soul is here, and though apparently absent, yet present in the highest and the truest sense. . . . Take good care of yourself, Austin, and think much of us all, for we do so of you.

EMILIE.

Several subsequent letters, all piquant and breezy, but dealing quite entirely with family matters, experiences with callers, and other personal subjects, have been omitted.

[March 24, 1852.]

Wednesday Morn.

You would n't think it was spring, Austin, if you were at home this morning, for we had a great snow-storm yesterday, and things are all white this morning. It sounds funny enough to hear birds singing and sleigh-bells at a time. But it won't last long, so you need n't think 't will be winter at the time when you come home.

I waited a day or two, thinking I might hear from you, but you will be looking for me, and wondering where I am, so I sha'n't wait any longer. We 're rejoiced that you 're coming home — the first thing we said to father when he got out of the stage was to ask if you were coming. I was sure you would all the while, for father said ' of course you would,' he should ' consent to no other arrangement,' and as you say, Austin, ' what father says he means.' How very soon it will be now — why, when I really think of it, how near and how happy it is! My heart grows light so fast that I could mount a grass-hopper and gallop around the world, and not fatigue him any! The sugar weather holds on, and I do believe it will stay until you come. . . . ' Mrs S.' is very feeble ; ' can't bear allopathic treatment, can't have homœopathic, don't want hydropathic,' oh,

what a pickle she is in. Should n't think she would
deign to live, it is so decidedly vulgar! They have
not yet concluded where to move — Mrs W. will
perhaps obtain board in the celestial city, but I 'm
sure I can't imagine what will become of the rest.
. . . Much love from us all.

EMILIE.

[May 10, 1852.]

Monday Morning, 5 *o'c.*

DEAR AUSTIN, — . . . Vinnie will tell you all the
news, so I will take a little place to describe a thun-
der-shower which occurred yesterday afternoon, —
the very first of the season. Father and Vinnie
were at meeting, mother asleep in her room, and
I at work by my window on a 'Lyceum lecture.'
The air was really scorching, the sun red and hot,
and you know just how the birds sing before a thun-
der-storm, a sort of hurried and agitated song —
pretty soon it began to thunder, and the great
'cream-colored heads' peeped out of their windows. Then came the wind and rain, and I hurried
around the house to shut all the doors and windows. I wish you had seen it come, so cool and
so refreshing — and everything glistening from it as
with a golden dew — I thought of you all the time.
This morning is fair and delightful. You will awake
in dust, and with it the ceaseless din of the untiring
city. Would n't you change your dwelling for my
palace in the dew? Good-by for now. I shall see
you so soon.

E.

Mr Edward Dickinson was in Baltimore when the following letter was written, in attendance upon the Whig Convention which sought, unsuccessfully, the nomination of Daniel Webster for the presidency.

[Amherst, June 21, 1852.]

Sunday Morning.

. . . Father has not got home, and we don't know when to expect him.   We had a letter from him yesterday, but he did n't say when he should come.   He writes that he 'should think the whole world was there, and some from other worlds.' He says he meets a great many old friends and acquaintances, and forms a great many new ones — he writes in very fine spirits, and says he enjoys himself very much. . . . I wish you could have gone with him, you would have enjoyed it so, but I did not much suppose that selfish old school would let you. . . . Last week the Senior levee came off at the President's.   I believe Professor Haven is to give one soon — and there is to be a reception at Professor Tyler's next Tuesday evening which I shall attend.   You see Amherst is growing lively, and by the time you come everything will be in a buzz. . . . We all send you our love.

EMILIE.

[Amherst, July 23, 1852.]

Sunday Night.

. . . You'd better not come home; I say the law will have you, a pupil of the law o'ertaken by the law, and brought to condign punishment, — scene for angels and men, or rather for archangels, who being a little higher would seem to have a 'vantage so far as view's concerned. '*Are* you pretty comfortable, though,' — and are you deaf and dumb and gone to the asylum where such afflicted persons learn to hold their tongues?

The next time you are n't going to write me, I'd thank you to let me know — this kind of *protracted* insult is what no man can bear. Fight with me like a man — let me have fair shot, and you are *caput mortuum et cap-a-pie*, and that ends the business! If you really think I so deserve this silence, tell me why — how — I'll be a thorough scamp or else I won't be any, just which you prefer.

T—— of S——'s class went to Boston yesterday; it was in my heart to send an apple by him for your private use, but father overheard some of my intentions, and said they were 'rather small' — whether this remark was intended for the apple, or for my noble self I did not think to ask him; I rather think he intended to give us both a cut — however, he may not!

You are coming home on Wednesday, as perhaps you know, and I am very happy in prospect of your coming, and hope you want to see us as much as we do you. Mother makes nicer pies with reference to your coming, I arrange my thoughts in a convenient shape, Vinnie grows only perter and more pert day by day.

The horse is looking finely — better than in his life — by which you may think him dead unless I add *before*. The carriage stands in state all covered in the chaise-house — we have one foundling hen into whose young mind I seek to instil the fact that ' Massa is a-comin ! '

The garden is amazing — we have beets and beans, have had splendid potatoes for three weeks now. Old Amos weeds and hoes and has an oversight of all thoughtless vegetables. The apples are fine and large in spite of my impression that father called them ' small.'

Yesterday there was a fire. At about three in the afternoon Mr Kimberly's barn was discovered to be on fire ; the wind was blowing a gale directly from the west, and having had no rain, the roofs [were] as dry as stubble. Mr Palmer's house was charred — the little house of father's — and Mr Kimberly's also. The engine was broken, and it seemed for a little while as if the whole street must go ; the Kimberlys' barn was burnt down, and the house much charred and injured, though not at all destroyed — Mr Palmer's barn took fire, and Deacon Leland's also, but were extinguished with only part burned roofs. We all feel very thankful at such a narrow escape.

Father says there was never such imminent danger, and such miraculous escape.   Father and Mr Frink took charge of the fire — or rather of the *water*, since fire usually takes care of itself.   The men all worked like heroes, and after the fire was out father gave commands to have them march to Howe's where an entertainment was provided for them. After the whole was over they gave 'three cheers for Edward Dickinson,' and three more for the insurance company.   On the whole, it is very wonderful that we did n't all burn up, and we ought to hold our tongues and be very thankful.   If there *must* be a fire, I 'm sorry it could n't wait until you had got home, because you seem to enjoy such things so very much.

There is nothing of moment now which I can find to tell you, except a case of measles in Hartford. . . . Good-by, Sir.   Fare you well.   My benison to your school.

[Amherst, Spring, 1853.]

Tuesday Noon.

DEAR AUSTIN, — . . . How soon now you are coming, and how happy we are in the thought of seeing you !   I can't realize that you will come, it is so still and lonely it does n't seem possible it can be otherwise ; but we shall see, when the nails hang full of coats again, and the chairs hang full of hats, and I can count the slippers under the chair.   Oh, Austin, how we miss them all, and more than them, some-

body who used to hang them there, and get many a hint ungentle to carry them away. Those times seem far off now, a great way, as things we did when children. I wish we were children now — I wish we were always children, how to grow up I don't know.
. . . Cousin J. has made us an Æolian harp which plays beautifully whenever there is a breeze.

Austin, you must n't care if your letters do not get here just when you think they will — they are always new to us, and delightful always, and the more you send us the happier we shall be. We all send our love to you, and think much and say much of seeing you again — keep well till you come, and if knowing that we all love you makes you happier, then, Austin, you may sing the whole day long !

Affectionately,

EMILIE.

[Amherst, March 18, 1853.]
Friday Morning.

DEAR AUSTIN, — I presume you remember a story that Vinnie tells of a breach of promise case where the correspondence between the parties consisted of a reply from the girl to one she had never received but was daily expecting. Well, *I* am writing an answer to the letter I have n't had, so you will see the force of the accompanying anecdote. I have been looking for you ever since despatching my last, but this is a fickle world, and it 's a great source of complacency that 't will all be burned up by and by. I should be pleased with a line when you 've published your work to father, if it 's perfectly convenient !

Your letters are very funny indeed — about the only jokes we have, now you are gone, and I hope you will send us one as often as you can. Father takes great delight in your remarks to him — puts on his spectacles and reads them o'er and o'er as if it was a blessing to have an only son. He reads all the letters you write, as soon as he gets them, at the post-office, no matter to whom addressed; then he makes me read them aloud at the supper table again, and when he gets home in the evening, he cracks a few walnuts, puts his spectacles on, and with your last in his hand, sits down to enjoy the evening. . . . I believe at this moment, Austin, that there 's nobody living for whom father has such respect as for you. But my paper is getting low, and I must hasten to tell you that we are very happy to hear good news from you, that we hope you 'll have pleasant times and learn a great deal while you 're gone, and come back to us greater and happier for the life lived at Cambridge. We miss you more and more. I wish that we could see you, but letters come the next — write them often, and tell us everything.

Affectionately,

EMILIE.

[June 14, 1853.]

. . . We have been free from company by the 'Amherst and Belchertown Railroad' since J. went home, though we live in constant fear of some other visitation. 'Oh, would some power the giftie gie' folks to see themselves as we see them. — *Burns*.

I have read the poems, Austin, and am going to read them again. They please me very much, but I must read them again before I know just what I think of 'Alexander Smith.' They are not very coherent, but there 's a good deal of exquisite frenzy, and some wonderful figures as ever I met in my life. We will talk about it again. The grove looks nicely, Austin, and we think must certainly grow. We love to go there — it is a charming place. Everything is singing now, and everything is beautiful that *can* be in its life. . . . The time for the New London trip has not been fixed upon. I sincerely wish it may wait until you get home from Cambridge if you would like to go.

The cars continue thriving — a good many passengers seem to arrive from somewhere, though nobody knows from where. Father expects his new buggy to arrive by the cars every day now, and that will help a little. I expect all our grandfathers and all their country cousins will come here to spend Commencement, and don't doubt the stock will rise several per cent that week. If we children could obtain board for the week in some 'vast wilderness,'

I think we should have good times. Our house is crowded daily with the members of this world, the high and the low, the bond and the free, the 'poor in this world's goods,' and the 'almighty dollar;' and what in the world they are after continues to be unknown. But I hope they will pass away as insects or vegetation, and let us reap together in golden harvest time. You and I and our sister Vinnie must have a pleasant time to be unmolested together when your school-days end. You must come home from school, not stopping to play by the way. . . . We all send our love to you, and miss you very much, and think of seeing you again very much. Write me again soon. I have said a good deal to-day.

EMILIE.

The new railroad was opened for the first regular trip from Palmer to Amherst, May 9, 1853. Mr Edward Dickinson wrote on that day, 'We have no railroad jubilee till we see whether all moves right, then we shall glorify becomingly.' Everything was apparently satisfactory, for the celebration occurred early in June, when more than three hundred New London people visited Amherst. In the following letter from Emily are indications of her growing distaste to mingle in a social *mêlée*, despite genuine interest in itself and its cause.

[June 20, 1853.]

Monday Morning.

MY DEAR AUSTIN, — . . . The New London day passed off grandly, so all the people said. It was pretty hot and dusty, but nobody cared for that. Father was, as usual, chief marshal of the day, and went marching around with New London at his heels like some old Roman general upon a triumph day. Mrs H. got a capital dinner, and was very much praised. Carriages flew like sparks, hither and thither and yon, and they all said 't was fine. I 'spose' it was. I sat in Professor Tyler's woods and saw the train move off, and then came home again for fear somebody would see me, or ask me how I did. Dr Holland was here, and called to see us — was very pleasant indeed, inquired for you, and asked mother if Vinnie and I might come and see them in Springfield. . . . We all send you our love.

EMILIE.

[Postmarked, July 2, 1853.]

Friday Afternoon.

DEAR AUSTIN, — . . . Some of the letters you 've sent us we have received, and thank you for affectionately. Some we have not received, but thank you for the memory, of which the emblem perished. Where all those letters go, yours and ours, somebody surely knows, but we do not. There 's a new postmaster to-day, but we don't know who 's to blame.

You never wrote me a letter, Austin, which I liked half so well as the one father brought me. We think of your coming home with a great deal of happiness, and are glad you want to come.

Father said he never saw you looking in better health or seeming in finer spirits. He did n't say a word about the Hippodrome or the Museum, and he came home so stern that none of us dared to ask him, and besides grandmother was here, and you certainly don't think I'd allude to a Hippodrome in the presence of that lady! I'd as soon think of popping fire-crackers in the presence of Peter the Great. But you'll tell us when you get home — how soon — how soon! . . . I admire the 'Poems' very much. We all send our love to you — shall write you again Sunday.

EMILIE.

[Summer, 1853.]

Sunday Afternoon.

. . . It is cold here to-day, Austin, and the west wind blows — the windows are shut at home, and the fire burns in the kitchen. How we should love to see you — how pleasant it would be to walk to the grove together. We will walk there when you get home. We all went down this morning, and the trees look beautifully — every one is growing, and when the west wind blows, the pines lift their light leaves and make sweet music. Pussy goes down there too, and seems to enjoy much in her own observations.

Mr Dwight has not answered yet; he probably will this week. I do think he will come, Austin, and shall be so glad if he will. . . . We all wish you here always, but I hope 't will seem only dearer for missing it so long. Father says you will come in three weeks — that won't be long now — keep well and happy, Austin, and remember us all you can, and much love from home and

EMILIE.

Thursday Evening.

. . . G. H. has just retired from an evening's visit here, and I gather my spent energies to write a word to you.

'Blessed are they that are persecuted for right-eousness' sake, for they shall have their reward!' Dear Austin, I don't *feel* funny, and I hope you won't laugh at anything I say. I am thinking of you and Vinnie — what nice times you are having, sitting and talking together, while I am lonely here, and I *wanted* to sit and think of you, and fancy what you were saying, all the evening long, but — ordained otherwise. I hope you will have grand times, and don't forget the unit without you, at home.

I have had some things from you to which I perceive no meaning. They either were very vast, or they didn't mean anything, I don't know certainly which. What did you mean by a note you sent me day before yesterday? Father asked me what you

wrote, and I gave it to him to read. He looked very
much confused, and finally put on his spectacles,
which did n't seem to help him much — I don't
think a telescope would have assisted him. I hope
you will write to me — I love to hear from you, and
now Vinnie is gone I shall feel very lonely. . . .
Love for them all if there are those to love and
think of me, and more and most for you, from

EMILY.

Tuesday Evening.

Well, Austin, dear Austin, you have got back
again, codfish and pork and all — all but the slippers, so nicely wrapped to take, yet found when
you were gone under the kitchen chair. I hope you
won't want them. Perhaps you have some more
there — I will send them by opportunity, should
there be such a thing. Vinnie proposed franking
them, but I fear they are rather large ! What should
you think of it? It is n't every day that we have a
chance to sponge Congress, . . . but Cæsar is such
'an honorable man' that we may all go to the poor-
house for all the American Congress will lift a finger
to help us. . . .

The usual rush of callers, and this beleaguered
family as yet in want of time. I do hope immortality will last a little while, but if the A——s
should happen to get there first, we shall be driven
there. . . .

EMILIE.

[March 17, 1854.]

. . . Since you went back to Cambridge the weather has been wonderful, — the thermometer every noon between 60 and 70 above zero, and the air full of birds.

To-day has not seemed like a day. It has been most unearthly, — so mild, so bright, so still, the windows open, and fires uncomfortable.

Since supper it lightens frequently. In the south you can see the lightning — in the north the northern lights. Now a furious wind blows just from the north and west, and winter comes back again. . . .

There is to be a party at Professor Haven's to-morrow night, for married people merely. Celibacy excludes me and my sister. Father and mother are invited. Mother will go. . . . Mother and Vinnie send love. They are both getting ready for Washington. Take care of yourself.

EMILIE.

Already Emily seems to have exhibited disinclination for journeys, as, in a letter to his son in Cambridge, dated at Washington, March 13, 1854, Mr Edward Dickinson said, ' I have written home to have Lavinia come with your mother and you, and Emily, too, if she will, but that I will not insist upon her coming.' Emily, however, did go to Washington with her family, later in the spring, as a subsequent letter to Mrs Holland will show.

[Amherst, March 27, 1854.]

Sunday Evening.

Well, Austin, — it's Sunday evening. Vinnie is
sick with the ague — mother taking a tour of the
second story as she is wont, Sabbath evening — the
wind is blowing high, the weather very cold, and I
am rather cast down in view of all these circumstances. . . . I went to meeting alone all day. I
assure you I felt very solemn. I went to meeting
five minutes before the bell rang, morning and afternoon, so not to have to go in after all the people
had got there. I wish you had heard Mr Dwight's
sermons to-day. He has preached wonderfully, and
I thought all the afternoon how I wished you were
there. . . . I will tell you something funny. You
know Vinnie sent father [at Washington] a box of
maple sugar — she got the box at the store, and it
said on the outside of it, '1 doz. genuine Quaker
Soap.' We did n't hear from the box, and so many
days passed we began to feel anxious lest it had never
reached him; and mother, writing soon, alluded in
her letter to the 'sugar sent by the girls,' and the
funniest letter from father came in answer to hers.
It seems the box went straightway, but father not
knowing the hand, merely took off the papers in
which the box was wrapped, and the label 'Quaker
Soap' so far imposed upon him that he put the box
in a drawer with his shaving materials, and supposed
himself well stocked with an excellent Quaker Soap.

. . . We all send our love to you, and want you should write us often.   Good-night, from

EMILIE.

. . . The Germanians gave a concert here the evening of exhibition day.   Vinnie and I went with J.   I never heard sounds before.   They seemed like brazen robins, all wearing broadcloth wings, and I think they were, for they all flew away as soon as the concert was over.

[Late Spring, 1854.]

Saturday Noon.

DEAR AUSTIN, — I rather thought from your letter to me that my essays, together with the lectures at Cambridge, were too much for you, so I thought I would let you have a little vacation; but you must have got rested now, so I shall renew the series.   Father was very severe to me; he thought I'd been trifling with you, so he gave me quite a trimming about 'Uncle Tom' and 'Charles Dickens' and these 'modern literati' who, he says, are nothing, compared to past generations who flourished when he was a boy.   Then he said there were 'somebody's rev-e-ries,' he did n't know whose they were, that he thought were very ridiculous — so I'm quite in disgrace at present, but I think of that 'pinnacle' on which you always mount when anybody insults you, and that's quite a comfort to me. . . .

After a page or two of information about friends in the village, the letter continues:

This is all the news I can think of, but there is one old story, Austin, which you may like to hear — it is that we think about you the whole of the live-long day, and talk of you when we 're together. And you can recollect when you are busy studying that those of us at home not so hard at work as you are, get much time to be with you. We all send our love to you.

EMILIE.

[Amherst, May, 1854.]

Saturday Morn.

DEAR AUSTIN, — A week ago we were all here — to-day we are not all here — yet the bee hums just as merrily, and all the busy things work on as if the same. They do not miss you, child, but there is a humming-bee whose song is not so merry, and there are busy ones who pause to drop a tear. Let us thank God, to-day, Austin, that we can love our friends, our brothers and our sisters, and weep when they are gone, and smile at their return. It is indeed a joy which we are blest to know.

To-day is very beautiful — just as bright, just as blue, just as green and as white and as crimson as the cherry-trees full in bloom, and the half-opening peach-blossoms, and the grass just waving, and sky and hill and cloud can make it, if they try. How I wish you were here, Austin; you thought last Saturday beautiful, yet to this golden day 't was but one single gem to whole handfuls of jewels. You will ride to-day, I hope, or take a long walk somewhere, and recollect us all, — Vinnie and me and father and mother and home. Yes, Austin, every one of us, for we all think of you, and bring you to recollection many times each day — not bring you to recollection, for we never put you away, but keep recollecting on. . . .

You must think of us to-night while Mr Dwight takes tea here, and we will think of you far away down in Cambridge.

Don't mind the can, Austin, if it is rather dry, don't mind the daily road though it is rather dusty, but remember the brooks and the hills, and remember while you 're but one, we are but four at home !

EMILIE.

CHAPTER III

To Mrs Gordon L. Ford, Mr Bowdoin, Mrs Anthon, and Miss Lavinia Dickinson

WITH a number of early letters to herself, Mrs Ford of Brooklyn sent me also a short sketch of her remembrance of Emily Dickinson's girlhood, which seems to show her in a somewhat different aspect from anything which other friends have given.

Mrs Ford was a daughter of the late Professor Fowler of Amherst College, and her recollections, making a pleasant picture of life in Amherst nearly fifty years ago, have all the charm of early friendship and intercourse in the days when plain living and high thinking were not an exceptional combination.

In speaking of several letters which she could not find, Mrs Ford wrote, 'The other things which I wish I could put my hand on were funny — sparkling with fun, and that is a new phase to the public; but she certainly began as a humorist.' Although sent to me for publication in this volume of *Letters*,

Mrs Ford had hoped to revise and perhaps shorten the sketch in the proof; and her sudden death, within a few days after writing it, lends a saddened interest to these memories of a vanished friendship.

'My remembrances of my friend Emily Dickinson are many and vivid, and delightful to me personally, yet they are all of trifles in themselves, and only interesting to the general public as they cast light on the growth and changes in her soul.

'Our parents were friends, and we knew each other from childhood, but she was several years younger, and how and when we drew together I cannot recall, but I think the friendship was based on certain sympathies and mutual admirations of beauty in nature and ideas. She loved the great aspects of nature, and yet was full of interest and affection for its smaller details. We often walked together over the lovely hills of Amherst, and I remember especially two excursions to Mount Norwottock, five miles away, where we found the climbing fern, and came home laden with pink and white trilliums, and later, yellow lady's-slippers. She knew the wood-lore of the region round about, and could name the haunts and the habits of every wild or garden growth within her reach. Her eyes were wide open to nature's sights, and her ears to nature's voices.

' My chief recollections of her are connected with these woodland walks, or out-door excursions with a merry party, perhaps to Sunderland for the "sugaring off" of the maple sap, or to some wild brook in the deeper forest, where the successful fishermen would afterward cook the chowder. She was a free talker about what interested her, yet I cannot remember one personal opinion expressed of her mates, her home, or her habits.

' Later we met to discuss books. *The Atlantic Monthly* was a youngster then, and our joy over a new poem by Lowell, Longfellow, and Whittier, our puzzles over Emerson's "If the red slayer think he slays," our laughter at Oliver Wendell Holmes, were full and satisfying. Lowell was especially dear to us, and once I saw a passionate fit of crying brought on, when a tutor of the College, who died while contesting the senatorship for Louisiana,[1] told us from his eight years of seniority, that "Byron had a much

[1] The Hon. Henry M. Spofford, Justice of the Supreme Court of Louisiana, a graduate of Amherst College in the Class of 1840, and brother of Mr Ainsworth R. Spofford, the Librarian of Congress.

better style," and advised us "to leave Lowell,
Motherwell and Emerson alone." Like other
young creatures, we were ardent partisans.

'There was a fine circle of young people
in Amherst, and we influenced each other
strongly. We were in the adoring mood, and
I am glad to say that many of those idols of
our girlhood have proved themselves golden.
The eight girls who composed this group had
talent enough for twice their number, and in
their respective spheres of mothers, authors
or women, have been noteworthy and admi-
rable. Three of them have passed from earth,
but the others live in activity and usefulness.

'This group started a little paper in the
Academy, now the village High School, which
was kept up for two years. Emily Dickinson
was one of the wits of the school, and a
humorist of the "comic column." Fanny
Montague often made the head title of the
paper — *Forest Leaves* — in leaves copied
from nature, and fantasies of her own pen-
work. She is now a wise member of art
circles in Baltimore, a manager of the Museum
of Art, and the appointed and intelligent critic
of the Japanese exhibit at the Exposition in
Chicago. Helen Fiske (the "H. H." of later
days) did no special work on the paper for
various reasons.

'This paper was all in script, and was passed around the school, where the contributions were easily recognized from the handwriting, which in Emily's case was very beautiful — small, clear, and finished. Later, though her writing retained its elegance, it became difficult to read. I wish very much I could find a copy of *Forest Leaves*, but we recklessly gave the numbers away, and the last one I ever saw turned up at the Maplewood Institute in Pittsfield, Massachusetts, where they started a similar paper. Emily's contributions were irresistible, but I cannot recall them. One bit was stolen by a roguish editor for the College paper, where her touch was instantly recognized; and there were two paragraphs in *The Springfield Republican.*

'We had a Shakespeare Club — a rare thing in those days, — and one of the tutors proposed to take all the copies of all the members and mark out the questionable passages. This plan was negatived at the first meeting, as far as "the girls" spoke, who said they did not want the strange things emphasized, nor their books spoiled with marks. Finally we told the men to do as they liked — "we shall read everything." I remember the lofty air with which Emily took her departure, saying, "There's nothing wicked in Shakespeare, and if there is I don't want to know it." The men read for perhaps three meetings from their expurgated editions, and then gave up their plan, and the whole text was read out boldly.

'There were many little dances, with cake and lemonade at the end, and one year there was a valentine party, where the lines of various authors were arranged to make apparent sense, but absolute nonsense, the play being to guess the names and places of the misappropriated lines.

'Emily was part and parcel of all these gatherings, and there were no signs, in her life and character, of the future recluse. As a prophetic hint, she once asked me if it did not make me shiver to hear a great many people talk — they took "all the clothes off their souls" — and we discussed this matter. She mingled freely in all the companies and excursions of the moment, and the evening frolics.

'Several of this group had beauty, all had intelligence and character, and others had charm. Emily was not beautiful, yet she had great beauties. Her eyes were lovely auburn, soft and warm, her hair lay in rings of the same color all over her head, and her skin and teeth were fine. At this time she had a demure manner which brightened easily into fun where she felt at home, but among strangers she was rather shy, silent, and even deprecating. She was exquisitely neat and careful in her dress, and always had flowers about her, another pleasant habit of modernity.

'I have so many times seen her in the morning at work in her garden where everything throve under her hand, and wandering there at eventide, that she is perpetually associated in my mind with flowers — a flower herself, — especially as for years it was her habit to send me the first buds of the arbutus which we had often hung over together in the woods, joying in its fresh fragrance as the very breath of coming spring.

'My busy married life separated me from these friends of my youth, and intercourse with them has not been frequent; but I rejoice that my early years were passed in scenes of beautiful nature, and with these mates of simple life, high cultivation and noble ideals. In Emily as in others, there was a rare combination of fervor and simplicity, with good practical living, great conscience and directness of purpose. She loved with all her might, there was never a touch of the worldling about her, and we all knew and trusted her love.

'Dr Holland once said to me, " Her poems are too ethereal for publication." I replied,

"They are beautiful — so concentrated — but they remind me of air-plants that have no roots in earth." "That is true," he said, "a perfect description;" and I think these lyrical ejaculations, these breathed-out projectiles, sharp as lances, would at that time have fallen into idle ears. But gathered in a volume where many could be read at once as her philosophy of life, they explain each other, and so become intelligible and delightful to the public.

'The first poem I ever read was the robin chorister[1] (published in the first volume) which she gave my husband years ago. I think in spite of her seclusion, she was longing for poetic sympathy, and that some of her later habits of life originated in this suppressed and ungratified desire.

'I only wish the interest and delight her poems have aroused could have come early enough in her career to have kept her social and communicative, and at one with her friends. Still, these late tributes to her memory are most welcome to the circle that loved her, even though they are but laurels to lay on her grave.

'E. E. F.'

---

[1] 'Some keep the Sabbath going to church,' etc.

The first letter was written in 1848; the others at intervals until 1853. Though placed in order, they were not dated by Mrs Ford.

[1848.]

DEAR EMILY, — I said when the barber came I would save you a little lock, and fulfilling my promise, I send you one to-day. I shall never give you anything again that will be half so full of sunshine as this wee lock of hair, but I wish no hue more sombre might ever fall to you.

All your gifts should be rainbows if I owned half the shine, and but a bit of sea to furnish raindrops for one. Dear Emily, this is all — it will serve to make you remember me when locks are crisp and gray, and the quiet cap, and the spectacles, and ‘John Anderson my Jo’ are all that is left of you.

I must have one of yours. Please spare me a little lock sometime when you have your scissors and there is one to spare.

Your very affectionate

EMILIE.

The buds are small, dear Emily, but will you please accept one for your cousin and yourself? I quite forgot the rosebugs when I spoke of the buds, last evening, and I found a family of them taking an early breakfast on my most precious bud, with a smart little worm for landlady, so the sweetest are gone, but accept my love with the smallest, and I 'm

Your affectionate

EMILIE.

Tuesday Morn.

DEAR EMILY, — I come and see you a great many times every day, though I don't bring my body with me, so perhaps you don't know I'm there. But I love to come just as dearly, for nobody sees me then, and I sit and chat away, and look up in your face, and no matter who calls if 'my Lord the King,' he does n't interrupt me. Let me say, dear Emily, both mean to come at a time, so you shall be very sure I am sitting by your side, and not have to trust the fancy. . . .

Affectionately,

E.

[1849 ?]

Thursday Morning.

DEAR EMILY, — I fear you will be lonely this dark and stormy day, and I send this little messenger to say you must not be.

The day is long to me. I have wanted to come and see you. I have tried earnestly to come, but always have been detained by some ungenerous care, and now this falling snow sternly and silently lifts up its hand between.

How glad I am affection can always leave and go. How glad that the drifts of snow pause at the outer door and go no farther, and it is as warm within as if no winter came. . . . Let us think of the pleas-ant summer whose gardens are far away, and whose robins are singing always. If it were not for blos-soms . . . and for that brighter sunshine above, beyond, away, these days were dark indeed; but I try to keep recollecting that we are away from home, and have many brothers and sisters who are expecting us. Dear Emilie, don't weep, for you will both be so happy where 'sorrow cannot come.'

Vinnie left her Testament on a little stand in our room, and it made me think of her, so I thought I would open it, and the first words I read were in those sweetest verses, ' Blessed are the poor — Blessed are they that mourn — Blessed are they that weep, for they shall be comforted.' Dear Emily, I thought of you, and I hastened away to send this message to you.

EMILIE.

Thursday Morn.

DEAR EMILY, — I can't come in this morning, because I am so cold, but you will know I am here ringing the big front door-bell, and leaving a note for you.

Oh, I want to come in, I have a great mind now to follow little Jane into your warm sitting-room; are you there, dear Emily?

No, I resist temptation and run away from the door just as fast as my feet will carry me, lest if I once come in I shall grow so happy that I shall stay there always and never go home at all. You will have read this note by the time I reach the office, and you can't think how fast I run.

Affectionately,

EMILY.

P. S. I have just shot past the corner, and now all the wayside houses, and the little gate flies open to see me coming home.

Saturday Morn.

It has been a long week, dear Emily, for I have not seen your face, but I have contrived to think of you very much instead, which has half reconciled me to not seeing you for so long. I was coming several times, but the snow would start the first, and then the paths were damp, and then a friend would drop in to chat, and the short afternoon was gone before I was aware.

Did Mr D—— give you a message from me? He promised to be faithful, but I don't suppose divines think earthly loves of much consequence. My flowers come in my stead to-day, dear Emily. I hope you will love to see them, and whatever word of love or welcome kindly you would extend to me, 'do even so to them.' They are small, but so full of meaning if they only mean the half of what I bid them.

Very affectionately,

EMILY.

Thursday Morning.

. . . When I am as old as you, and have had so many friends, perhaps they won't seem so precious, and then I sha'n't write any more little *billets-doux* like these, but you will forgive me now, because I can't find many so dear to me as you. Then I know I can't have you always; some day a 'brave dra-

goon' will be stealing you away, and I will have
farther to go to discover you at all, so I shall recollect all these sweet opportunities, and feel so sorry if
I did n't improve them. . . .

About this time (December, 1849), the following little note was sent to Mr Bowdoin, a
law student in Mr Dickinson's office; 'on returning *Jane Eyre*. The leaves mentioned
were box leaves.'

[December, 1849.]

Mr Bowdoin, — If all these leaves were altars,
and on every one a prayer that Currer Bell might be
saved, and you were God — would you answer it?

Mr Bowdoin, who was considered by the
young girls at that time 'a confirmed bache-
lor,' also received the accompanying valentine
from Emily.

Valentine Week [1850].

Awake, ye muses nine, sing me a strain divine,
Unwind the solemn twine, and tie my Valentine.

.   .   .   .

Oh the earth was *made* for lovers, for damsel, and
　　hopeless swain,
For sighing, and gentle whispering, and *unity* made
　　of *twain*.
All things do go a courting, in earth or sea, or air,
God hath made nothing single but *thee* in His world
　　so fair !

The *bride* and then the *bridegroom*, the *two*, and
    then the *one*,
Adam, and Eve, his consort, the moon and then the
    sun;
The life doth prove the precept, who obey shall
    happy be,
Who will not serve the sovereign, be hanged on fatal
    tree.
The high do seek the lowly, the great do seek the
    small,
None cannot find who seeketh, on this terrestrial
    ball;
The bee doth court the flower, the flower his suit
    receives,
And they make a merry wedding, whose guests are
    hundred leaves;
The wind doth woo the branches, the branches they
    are won,
And the father fond demandeth the maiden for his
    son.
The storm doth walk the seashore humming a mourn-
    ful tune,
The wave with eye so pensive, looketh to see the
    moon,
Their spirits meet together, they make them solemn
    vows,
No more he singeth mournful, her sadness she doth
    lose.
The worm doth woo the mortal, death claims a living
    bride,

Night unto day is married, morn unto eventide;
Earth is a merry damsel, and heaven a knight so
  true,
And Earth is quite coquettish, and beseemeth in vain
  to sue.
Now to the application, to the reading of the roll,
To bringing thee to justice, and marshalling thy soul:
Thou art a *human* solo, a being cold, and lone,
Wilt have no kind companion, thou reapest what
  thou hast sown.
Hast never silent hours, and minutes all too long,
And a deal of sad reflection, and wailing instead of
  song?
There 's *Sarah*, and *Eliza*, and *Emeline* so fair,
And *Harriet* and *Sabra*, and she with curling hair.
Thine eyes are sadly blinded, but yet thou mayest
  see
Six true and comely maidens sitting upon the tree;
Approach that tree with caution, then up it boldly
  climb,
And seize the one thou lovest, nor care for space, or
  time.
Then bear her to the greenwood, and build for her
  a bower,
And give her what she asketh, jewel, or bird, or
  flower —
And bring the fife, and trumpet, and beat upon the
  drum —
And bid the world Goodmorrow, and go to glory
  home!

Valentines seemed ever near the thoughts
of the young people of this generation, and
another clever one, written by Emily in 1852,
somehow found its way into *The Republican*,
probably through some friend. It was origi-
nally sent to Mr William Howland.

[1852.]

Sic transit gloria mundi,
How doth the busy bee —
Dum vivimus vivamus,
I stay mine enemy.

Oh, *veni, vidi, vici,*
Oh, *caput, cap-a-pie,*
And oh, *memento mori*
When I am far from thee.

Hurrah for Peter Parley,
Hurrah for Daniel Boone,
Three cheers, sir, for the gentlemen
Who first observed the moon.

Peter put up the sunshine,
Pattie arrange the stars,
Tell Luna tea is waiting,
And call your brother Mars.

Put down the apple, Adam,
And come away with me ;
So shall thou have a pippin
From off my father's tree.

I climb the hill of science
I ' view the landscape o'er,'
Such transcendental prospect
I ne'er beheld before.

Unto the Legislature
My country bids me go.
I 'll take my india-rubbers,
In case the wind should blow.

During my education,
It was announced to me
That gravitation, stumbling,
Fell from an apple-tree.

The earth upon its axis
Was once supposed to turn,
By way of a gymnastic
In honor to the sun.

It was the brave Columbus,
A-sailing on the tide,
Who notified the nations
Of where I would reside.

Mortality is fatal,
Gentility is fine,
Rascality heroic,
Insolvency sublime.

Our fathers being weary
Lay down on Bunker Hill,
And though full many a morning,
Yet they are sleeping still.

The trumpet, sir, shall wake them,
In dream I see them rise,
Each with a solemn musket
A-marching to the skies.

A coward will remain, sir,
Until the fight is done,
But an immortal hero
Will take his hat and run.

Good-by, sir, I am going —
My country calleth me.
Allow me, sir, at parting
To wipe my weeping e'e.

In token of our friendship
Accept this *Bonnie Doon,*
And when the hand that plucked it
Has passed beyond the moon,

The memory of my ashes
Will consolation be.
Then farewell, Tuscarora,
And farewell, sir, to thee.

To Mrs Ford.

Sunday Afternoon [1852].

I have just come home from meeting, where I
have been all day, and it makes me so happy to
think of writing you that I forget the sermon and

minister and all, and think of none but you. . . .
I miss you always, dear Emily, and I think now and
then that I can't stay without you, and half make
up my mind to make a little bundle of all my earthly
things, bid my blossoms and home good-by, and set
out on foot to find you. But we have so much
matter of fact here that I don't dare to go, so I keep
on sighing, and wishing you were here.

I know you would be happier amid this darling
spring than in ever so kind a city, and you would get
well much faster drinking our morning dew — and
the world here is so beautiful, and things so sweet
and fair, that your heart would be soothed and
comforted.

I would tell you about the spring if I thought it
might persuade you even now to return, but every
bud and bird would only afflict you and make you
sad where you are, so not one word of the robins,
and not one word of the bloom, lest it make the
city darker, and your own home more dear.

But nothing forgets you, Emily, not a blossom, not
a bee ; for in the merriest flower there is a pensive
air, and in the bonniest bee a sorrow — they know
that you are gone, they know how well you loved
them, and in their little faces is sadness, and in their
mild eyes, tears. But another spring, dear friend,
you must and shall be here, and nobody can take
you away, for I will hide you and keep you — and
who would think of taking you if I hold you tight in
my arms?

Your home looks very silent — I try to think of things funny, and turn the other way when I am passing near, for sure I am that looking would make my heart too heavy, and make my eyes so dim. How I do long once more to hear the household voices, and see you there at twilight sitting in the door — and I shall when the leaves fall, sha'n't I, and the crickets begin to sing?

You must not think sad thoughts, dear Emily. I fear you are doing so, from your sweet note to me, and it almost breaks my heart to have you so far away, where I cannot comfort you.

All will be well, I know, and I know all will be happy, and I so wish I was near to convince my dear friend so. I want very much to hear how Mr Ford is now. I hope you will tell me, for it's a good many weeks since I have known anything of him. You and he may come this way any summer; and how I hope he may — and I shall pray for him, and for you, and for your home on earth, which will be next the one in heaven.

Your very affectionate,

EMILIE.

I thank you for writing me, one precious little 'forget-me-not' to bloom along my way. But one little one is lonely — pray send it a blue-eyed mate, that it be not alone. Here is love from mother and father and Vinnie and me. . . .

[1853.]

Wednesday Eve.

DEAR EMILY, — Are you there, and shall you always stay there, and is it not dear Emily any more, but Mrs Ford of Connecticut, and must we stay alone, and will you not come back with the birds and the butterflies, when the days grow long and warm?

Dear Emily, we are lonely here. I know Col. S—— is left, and Mr and Mrs K——, but pussy has run away, and you do not come back again, and the world has grown so long! I knew you would go away, for I know the roses are gathered, but I guessed not yet, not till by expectation we had become resigned. Dear Emily, when it came, and hidden by your veil you stood before us all and made those promises, and when we kissed you, all, and went back to our homes, it seemed to me translation, not any earthly thing, and if a little after you'd ridden on the wind, it would not have surprised me.

And now five days have gone, Emily, and long and silent, and I begin to know that you will not come back again. There's a verse in the Bible, Emily, I don't know where it is, nor just how it goes can I remember, but it's a little like this — 'I can go to her, but she cannot come back to me.' I guess that isn't right, but my eyes are full of tears, and I'm sure I do not care if I make mistakes or not. Is it happy there, dear Emily, and is the fireside warm, and have you a little cricket to chirp upon the hearth?

How much we think of you — how dearly love you — how often hope for you that it may all be happy.

Sunday evening your father came in — he stayed a little while. I thought he looked solitary. I thought he had grown old. How lonely he must be — I'm sorry for him.

Mother and Vinnie send their love, and hope you are so happy. Austin has gone away. Father comes home to-morrow. I know father will miss you. He loved to meet you here.

> ' So fades a summer cloud away,
>   So smiles the gale when storms are o'er,
> So gently shuts the eye of day,
>   So dies a wave along the shore.'

Kiss me, dear Emily, and remember me if you will, with much respect, to your husband. Will you write me sometime?

Affectionately,

EMILY.

To Mrs Anthon.

AMHERST [1859].

. . . Sweet at my door this March night another candidate. Go home! We don't like Katies here! Stay! My heart votes for you, and what am I, indeed, to dispute her ballot!

What are your qualifications? Dare you dwell in the East where we dwell? Are you afraid of the sun? When you hear the new violet sucking her way among the sods, shall you be resolute? All we are strangers, dear, the world is not acquainted with us, because we are not acquainted with her; and pilgrims. Do you hesitate? And soldiers, oft — some of us victors, but those I do not see to-night, owing to the smoke. We are hungry, and thirsty, sometimes, we are barefoot and cold — will you still come?

Then, bright I record you — Kate, gathered in March! It is a small bouquet, dear, but what it lacks in size it gains in fadelessness. Many can boast a hollyhock, but few can bear a rose! And should new flower smile at limited associates, pray her remember were there many, they were not worn upon the breast, but tilled in the pasture. So I rise wearing her — so I sleep holding, — sleep at last with her fast in my hand, and wake bearing my flower.   EMILIE.

To the Same.

There are two ripenings, one of sight,
Whose forces spheric wind,
Until the velvet product
Drops spicy to the ground.
A homelier maturing,
A process in the burr
That teeth of frosts alone disclose
On far October air.
                                      EMILIE.

To the Same.

[1860.]

The prettiest of pleas, dear, but with a lynx like me quite unavailable. Finding is slow, facilities for losing so frequent, in a world like this, I hold with extreme caution. A prudence so astute may seem unnecessary, but plenty moves those most, dear, who have been in want, and Saviour tells us, Kate, the poor are always with us. Were you ever poor? I have been a beggar, and rich to-night, as by God's leave I believe I am, the 'lazzaroni's' faces haunt, pursue me still!

You do not yet 'dislimn,' Kate. Distinctly sweet your face stands in its phantom niche — I touch your hand — my cheek your cheek — I stroke your vanished hair. Why did you enter, sister, since you must depart? Had not its heart been torn enough but you must send your shred?

Oh, our condor Kate! Come from your crags again! Oh, dew upon the bloom fall yet again a summer's night! Of such have been the frauds which have vanquished faces, sown plant of flesh the church-yard plats, and occasioned angels.

There is a subject, dear, on which we never touch. Ignorance of its pageantries does not deter me. I too went out to meet the dust early in the morning. I too in daisy mounds possess hid treasure, therefore I guard you more. You did not tell me you had

once been a 'millionaire.' Did my sister think that
opulence could be mistaken? Some trinket will
remain, some babbling plate or jewel.

I write you from the summer. The murmuring
leaves fill up the chinks through which the winter red
shone when Kate was here, and F—— was here, and
frogs sincerer than our own splash in their Maker's
pools. It 's but a little past, dear, and yet how far
from here it seems, fled with the snow! So through
the snow go many loving feet parted by 'Alps.' How
brief, from vineyards and the sun!

Parents and Vinnie request love to be given girl.

                                    EMILIE.

[1861 ?]

To the Same.

KATIE, — Last year at this time I did not miss
you, but positions shifted, until I hold your black
in strong hallowed remembrance, and trust my colors
are to you tints slightly beloved.

You cease, indeed, to talk, which is a custom
prevalent among things parted and torn, but shall I
class this, dear, among elect exceptions, and bear
you just as usual unto the kind Lord?

We dignify our faith when we can cross the ocean
with it, though most prefer ships.

How do you do this year? . . . How many years,
I wonder, will sow the moss upon them, before we
bind again, a little altered, it may be, elder a little

it *will* be, and yet the same, as suns which shine between our lives and loss, and violets — not last year's, but having the mother's eyes.

Do you find plenty of food at home? Famine is unpleasant.

It is too late for frogs — or what pleases me better, dear, not quite early enough! The pools were full of you for a brief period, but that brief period blew away, leaving me with many stems, and but a few foliage! Gentlemen here have a way of plucking the tops of the trees, and putting the fields in their cellars annually, which in point of taste is execrable, and would they please omit, I should have fine vegetation and foliage all the year round, and never a winter month. Insanity to the sane seems so unnecessary — but I am only one, and they are 'four and forty,' which little affair of numbers leaves me impotent. Aside from this, dear Katie, inducements to visit Amherst are as they were — I am pleasantly located in the deep sea, but love will row you out, if her hands are strong, and don't wait till I land, for I'm going ashore on the other side.

EMILIE.

Following are letters written to her sister, Miss Lavinia Dickinson, while Emily was receiving treatment for her eyes in Boston. She was there for this purpose twice, — during the summer of 1864, and again in 1865, usually writing of these years as 'when I was sick so long,' which has given many persons the idea of an invalidism she never had.

[1864.]

DEAR VINNIE, — Many write that they do not write because that they have too much to say, I that I have enough. Do you remember the whippoorwill that sang one night on the orchard fence, and then drove to the south, and we never heard of him afterward?

He will go home, and I shall go home, perhaps in the same train. It is a very sober thing to keep my summer in strange towns — what, I have not told, but I have found friends in the wilderness. You know Elijah did, and to see the 'ravens' mending my stockings would break a heart long hard.

Fanny and Lou are solid gold, and Mrs B—— and her daughter very kind, and the doctor enthusiastic about my getting well. I feel no gayness yet — I suppose I had been discouraged so long.

You remember the prisoner of Chillon did not know liberty when it came, and asked to go back to jail.

C—— and A—— came to see me and brought beautiful flowers. Do you know what made them remember me? Give them my love and gratitude.

They told me about the day at Pelham, you, dressed in daisies, and Mr McD——. I could n't see you, Vinnie. I am glad of all the roses you find,

while your primrose is gone. How kind Mr C——
grew. Was Mr D—— dear?

Emily wants to be well — if any one alive wants
to get well more, I would let him, first.

Give my love to father and mother and Austin.
Tell Margaret I remember her, and hope Richard is
well. . . . How I wish I could rest all those who are
tired for me.

EMILY.

To the Same.

[1865.]

DEAR VINNIE, — The hood is far under way, and
the girls think it a beauty. . . . I hope the chimneys
are done, and the hemlocks set, and the two teeth
filled in the front yard.   How astonishing it will
be to me ! . . .

The pink lily you gave Lou has had five flowers
since I came, and has more buds.   The girls think
it my influence.   Lou wishes she knew father's view
of Jeff Davis' capture — thinks no one but him can
do it justice.   She wishes to send a photograph of
the arrest to Austin, including the skirt and spurs,
but fears he will think her trifling with him.   I
advised her not to be rash.

How glad I should be to see you all, but it won't
be long, Vinnie.   You will be willing, won't you, for
a little while?   It has rained and been very hot,
and mosquitoes, as in August.   I hope the flowers are
well.   The tea-rose I gave Aunt L—— has a flower

now.   Is the lettuce ripe? Persons wear no bonnets
here. Fanny has a blade of straw with handle of
ribbon.

Affectionately,

EMILY.

To the Same.

. . . Father told me you were going.   I wept for
the little plants, but rejoiced for you.   Had I loved
them as well as I did, I could have begged you to
stay with them, but they are foreigners now, and all,
a foreigner.   I have been sick so long I do not know
the sun.   I hope they may be alive, for home would
be strange except them, now the world is dead.

A—— N—— lives here since Saturday, and two
new people more, a person and his wife, so I do little
but fly, yet always find a nest. I shall go home in
two weeks. You will get me at Palmer?

Love for E—— and Mr D——.

SISTER.

To the Same.

. . . The Doctor will let me go Monday of Thanksgiving week. He wants to see me Sunday, so I cannot before. . . . . Love for the Middletown pearls.
Shall write E—— after Tuesday, when I go to the
Doctor. Thank her for sweet note.

The drums keep on for the still man — but Emily
must stop.

Love of Fanny and Lou.

SISTER.

Soon after the close of the war, a friend, Mrs Vanderbilt of Long Island, met with a very serious bodily accident. Upon her recovery she received the following welcome to the realm of health : —

> To this world she returned,
> But with a tingle of that ;
> A compound manner,
> As a sod
> Espoused a violet
> That chiefer to the skies
> Than to himself allied,
> Dwelt, hesitating,
> Half of dust,
> And half of day, the bride.
>
> EMILY.

On the occasion of another friend's departure from Amherst after a visit, Emily's good-by was embodied in the following lines, accompanied by an oleander blossom tied with black ribbon :

> We 'll pass without a parting,
> So to spare
> Certificate of absence,
> Deeming where
> I left her I could find her
> If I tried.
> This way I keep from missing
> Those who died.
>
> EMILY.

CHAPTER IV

To Dr J. G. Holland, and Mrs Holland

THE dates of these letters can be approximated only by the hand-writing — which varies from the early style, about 1853, to the latest — and by events mentioned, the time of whose occurrence is known. Mrs Holland writes that there were many other letters, even more quaint and original, but unhappily not preserved.

[About 1853.]

Friday Evening.

Thank you, dear Mrs Holland — Vinnie and I will come, if you would like to have us. We should have written before, but mother has not been well, and we hardly knew whether we could leave her, but she is better now, and I write quite late this evening, that if you still desire it, Vinnie and I will come. Then, dear Mrs Holland, if agreeable to you, we will take the Amherst train on Tuesday morning, for Springfield, and be with you at noon.

The cars leave here at nine o'clock, and I think

reach Springfield at twelve. I can think just how we dined with you a year ago from now, and it makes my heart beat faster to think perhaps we 'll see you so little while from now.

To live a thousand years would not make me forget the day and night we spent there, and while I write the words, I don't believe I 'm coming, so sweet it seems to me. I hope we shall not tire you ; with all your other cares, we fear we should not come, but you *will* not let us trouble you, will you, dear Mrs Holland?

Father and mother ask a very warm remembrance to yourself and Dr Holland.

We were happy the grapes and figs seemed acceptable to you, and wished there were many more. I am very sorry to hear that ' Kate ' has such excellent lungs. With all your other cares, it must be quite a trial to you.

It is also a source of pleasure to me that Annie goes to sleep, on account of the ' interregnum ' it must afford to you.

Three days and we are there — happy — very happy ! To-morrow I will sew, but I shall think of you, and Sunday sing and pray — yet I shall not forget you, and Monday 's very near, and here 's to me on Tuesday ! Good-night, dear Mrs Holland — I see I 'm getting wild — you will forgive me all, and not *forget* me all, though? Vinnie is fast asleep, or her love would be here — though she is, it is. Once more, if it is fair, we will come on Tuesday, and you love to have us, but if not convenient, please surely tell us so.

Affectionately,

EMILIE.

Tuesday Evening.

DEAR DR AND MRS HOLLAND, — dear Minnie — it is cold to-night, but the thought of you so warm, that I sit by it as a fireside, and am never cold any more. I love to write to you — it gives my heart a holiday and sets the bells to ringing. If prayers had any answers to them, you were all here to-night, but I seek and I don't find, and knock and it is not opened. Wonder if God is just — presume He is, however, and 't was only a blunder of Matthew's.

I think mine is the case, where when they ask an egg, they get a scorpion, for I keep wishing for you, keep shutting up my eyes and looking toward the sky, asking with all my might for you, and yet you do not come. I wrote to you last week, but thought you would laugh at me, and call me sentimental, so I kept my lofty letter for 'Adolphus Hawkins, Esq.'

If it was n't for broad daylight, and cooking-stoves, and roosters, I'm afraid you would have occasion to smile at my letters often, but so sure as 'this mortal' essays immortality, a crow from a neighboring farm-yard dissipates the illusion, and I am here again.

And what I mean is this — that I thought of you

all last week, until the world grew rounder than it sometimes is, and I broke several dishes.

Monday, I solemnly resolved I would be *sensible*, so I wore thick shoes, and thought of Dr Humphrey, and the Moral Law. One glimpse of *The Republican* makes me break things again — I read in it every night.

Who writes those funny accidents, where railroads meet each other unexpectedly, and gentlemen in factories get their heads cut off quite informally? The author, too, relates them in such a sprightly way, that they are quite attractive. Vinnie was disappointed to-night, that there were not more accidents — I read the news aloud, while Vinnie was sewing. *The Republican* seems to us like a letter from you, and we break the seal and read it eagerly. . . .

Vinnie and I talked of you as we sewed, this afternoon. I said — 'how far they seem from us,' but Vinnie answered me 'only a little way.' . . . I'd love to be a bird or bee, that whether hum or sing, still might be near you.

Heaven is large — is it not? Life is short too, isn't it? Then when one is done, is there not another, and — and — then if God is willing, we are neighbors then. Vinnie and mother send their love. Mine too is here. My letter as a bee, goes laden. Please love us and remember us. Please write us very soon, and tell us how you are. . . .

Affectionately,

EMILIE.

Tuesday Evening

Dear Dr, and Mrs Holland —
dear Minnie — it is cold tonight,
but the thought of you so
warm, that I sit by it as a
fireside, and am never cold
any more. I love to write to you.
it gives my heart a holiday
and sets the bells to ringing.
If prayers had any answers to
them, you were all here tonight,
but I knock and I ask, and
and knock, and it is not stirred.
Wonder if God is just — presume
he is however, and 'twas one
a blunder of Matthew's?

Aff, Emily —

[Late Autumn, 1853.]

Sabbath Afternoon.

DEAR FRIENDS, — I thought I would write again.
I write you many letters with pens which are not
seen. Do you receive them?

I think of you all to-day, and dreamed of you last
night.

When father rapped on my door to wake me this
morning, I was walking with you in the most wonderful garden, and helping you pick — roses, and
though we gathered with all our might, the basket
was never full. And so all day I pray that I may
walk with you, and gather roses again, and as night
draws on, it pleases me, and I count impatiently
the hours 'tween me and the darkness, and the
dream of you and the roses, and the basket never
full.

God grant the basket fill not, till, with hands purer
and whiter, we gather flowers of gold in baskets
made of pearl; higher — higher! It seems long
since we heard from you — long, since how little
Annie was, or any one of you — so long since Cattle
Show, when Dr Holland was with us. Oh, it always
seems a long while from our seeing you, and even
when at your house, the nights seemed much more
long than they 're wont to do, because separated
from you. I want so much to know if the friends
are all well in that dear cot in Springfield — and if
well whether happy, and happy — *how* happy, and

why, and what bestows the joy? And then those other questions, asked again and again, whose answers are so sweet, do they love — remember us — wish sometimes we were there? Ah, friends — dear friends — perhaps my queries tire you, but I so long to know.

The minister to-day, not our own minister, preached about death and judgment, and what would become of those, meaning Austin and me, who behaved improperly — and somehow the sermon scared me, and father and Vinnie looked very solemn as if the whole was true, and I would not for worlds have them know that it troubled me, but I longed to come to you, and tell you all about it, and learn how to be better. He preached such an awful sermon though, that I did n't much think I should ever see you again until the Judgment Day, and then you would not speak to me, according to his story. The subject of perdition seemed to please him, somehow. It seems very solemn to me. I 'll tell you all about it, when I see you again.

I wonder what you are doing to-day — if you have been to meeting? To-day has been a fair day, very still and blue. To-night the crimson children are playing in the west, and to-morrow will be colder. How sweet if I could see you, and talk of all these things! Please write us very soon. The days with you last September seem a great way off, and to meet you again, delightful. I 'm sure it won't be long before we sit together.

Then will I not repine, knowing that bird of mine, though flown — learneth beyond the sea, melody new for me, and will return.

Affectionately,

EMILY.

This little poem was enclosed in the fore-going letter: —

> Truth is as old as God,
> His twin identity —
> And will endure as long as He,
> A co-eternity,
> And perish on the day
> That He is borne away
> From mansion of the universe,
> A lifeless Deity.

[Enclosing some leaves, 1854.]

January 2d.

May it come *to-day* ?

Then New Year the sweetest, and long life the merriest, and the Heaven highest — by and by !

EMILIE.

[Spring, 1854.]

PHILADELPHIA.

DEAR MRS HOLLAND AND MINNIE, and Dr Holland too — I have stolen away from company to write a note to you ; and to say that I love you still.

I am not at home — I have been away just five

weeks to-day, and shall not go quite yet back to
Massachusetts. Vinnie is with me here, and we
have wandered together into many new ways.

We were three weeks in Washington, while father
was there, and have been two in Philadelphia. We
have had many pleasant times, and seen much that
is fair, and heard much that is wonderful — many
sweet ladies and noble gentlemen have taken us by
the hand and smiled upon us pleasantly — and the
sun shines brighter for our way thus far.

I will not tell you what I saw — the elegance,
the grandeur; you will not care to know the value of
the diamonds my Lord and Lady wore, but if you
have n't been to the sweet Mount Vernon, then I *will*
tell you how on one soft spring day we glided down
the Potomac in a painted boat, and jumped upon
the shore — how hand in hand we stole along up a
tangled pathway till we reached the tomb of General
George Washington, how we paused beside it, and
no one spoke a word, then hand in hand, walked
on again, not less wise or sad for that marble story;
how we went within the door — raised the latch
he lifted when he last went home — thank the Ones
in Light that he 's since passed in through a brighter
wicket! Oh, I could spend a long day, if it did not
weary you, telling of Mount Vernon — and I will
sometime if we live and meet again, and God grant
we shall!

I wonder if you have all forgotten us, we have
stayed away so long. I hope you have n't — I tried

to write so hard before I went from home, but the moments were so busy, and then they *flew* so.   I was sure when days *did* come in which I was less busy, I should seek your forgiveness, and it did not occur to me that you might not forgive me.   Am I too late to-day?   Even if you are angry, I shall keep praying you, till from very weariness, you will take me in.   It seems to me many a day since we were in Springfield, and Minnie and the *dumb-bells* seem as vague — as vague ; and sometimes I wonder if I ever dreamed — then if I'm dreaming now, then if I *always* dreamed, and there is not a world, and not these darling friends, for whom I would not count my life too great a sacrifice.   Thank God there is a world, and that the friends we love dwell forever and ever in a house above.   I fear I grow incongruous, but to meet my friends does delight me so that I quite forget time and sense and so forth.

Now, my precious friends, if you won't forget me until I get home, and become more sensible, I will write again, and more properly.   Why didn't I ask before, if you were well and happy?

Forgetful

EMILIE.

[November, 1854.]

Saturday Eve.

I come in flakes, dear Dr Holland, for verily it snows, and as descending swans, here a pinion and there a pinion, and anon a plume, come the bright inhabitants of the white home.

I know they fall in Springfield; perhaps you see them now — and therefore I look out again, to see if you are looking.

How pleasant it seemed to hear your voice — so said Vinnie and I, as we as individuals, and then collectively, read your brief note. Why did n't you speak to us before? We thought you had forgotten us — we concluded that one of the bright things had gone forever more. That is a sober feeling, and it must n't come too often in such a world as this. A violet came up next day, and blossomed in our garden, and were it not for these same flakes, I would go in the dark and get it, so to send to you. Thank Him who is in Heaven, Katie Holland lives! Kiss her on every cheek for me — I really can't remember how many the bairn has — and give my warmest recollection to Mrs Holland and Minnie, whom to love, this Saturday night, is no trifling thing. I 'm very happy that you are happy — and that you cheat the angels of another one.

I would the many households clad in dark attire had succeeded so. You must all be happy and strong and well. I love to have the lamps shine on your evening table. I love to have the sun shine on your daily walks.

The 'new house'! God bless it! You will leave the 'maiden and married life of Mary Powell' behind.

Love and remember   EMILIE.

While the family lived for many years in the old mansion built by Emily Dickinson's grandfather, the Hon. Samuel Fowler Dickinson, they had moved away from it about 1840; and the following letter describes their return after fifteen years to their early home, where Emily was born, and where she died: —

[1855.]

Sabbath Day.

Your voice is sweet, dear Mrs Holland — I wish I heard it oftener.

One of the mortal musics Jupiter denies, and when indeed its gentle measures fall upon my ear, I stop the birds to listen. Perhaps you think I *have* no bird, and this is rhetoric —. pray, Mr Whately, what is *that* upon the cherry-tree? Church is done, and the winds blow, and Vinnie is in that pallid land the simple call 'sleep.' They will be wiser by and by, we shall all be wiser! While I sit in the snows, the summer day on which you came and the bees and the south wind, seem fabulous as *Heaven* seems to a sinful world — and I keep remembering it till it assumes a *spectral* air, and nods and winks at me, and then all of you turn to phantoms and vanish slow away. We cannot talk and laugh more, in the parlor where we met, but we learned to love for aye, there, so it is just as well.

We shall sit in a parlor 'not made with hands' unless we are very careful!

I cannot tell you how we moved. I had rather not remember. I believe my 'effects' were brought in a bandbox, and the 'deathless me,' on foot, not many moments after. I took at the time a memorandum of my several senses, and also of my hat and coat, and my best shoes — but it was lost in the *mêlée*, and I am out with lanterns, looking for myself.

Such wits as I reserved, are so badly shattered that repair is useless — and still I can't help laughing at my own catastrophe. I supposed we were going to make a 'transit,' as heavenly bodies did — but we came budget by budget, as our fellows do, till we fulfilled the pantomime contained in the word 'moved.' It is a kind of *gone-to-Kansas* feeling, and if I sat in a long wagon, with my family tied behind, I should suppose without doubt I was a party of emigrants!

They say that 'home is where the heart is.' I think it is where the *house* is, and the adjacent buildings.

But, my dear Mrs Holland, I have another story, and lay my laughter all away, so that I can sigh. Mother has been an invalid since we came *home*, and Vinnie and I 'regulated,' and Vinnie and I 'got settled,' and still we keep our father's house, and mother lies upon the lounge, or sits in her easy-chair. I don't know what her sickness is, for I am but a simple child, and frightened at myself. I often wish I was a grass, or a toddling daisy, whom all these problems of the dust might not terrify — and should my own machinery get slightly out of gear, *please*, kind ladies and gentlemen, some one stop the wheel, — for I know that with belts and bands of gold, I shall whizz triumphant on the new stream ! Love for you — love for Dr Holland — thanks for his exquisite hymn — tears for your sister in sable, and kisses for Minnie and the bairns.

From your mad

EMILIE.

[Spring, 1856?]

. . . February passed like a skate and I know March. Here is the 'light' the stranger said 'was not on sea or land.' Myself could arrest it, but will not chagrin him.

. . . Cousin Peter told me the Doctor would address Commencement — trusting it insure you both for papa's *fête* I endowed Peter. We do not always know the source of the smile that flows to us. . . .

My flowers are near and foreign, and I have but to cross the floor to stand in the Spice Isles.

The wind blows gay to-day and the jays bark like blue terriers.

I tell you what I see — the landscape of the spirit requires a lung, but no tongue. I hold you few I

love, till my heart is red as February and purple as
March.

Hand for the Doctor.   EMILY.

[Late Summer, 1856.]

Sabbath Night.

Don't tell, dear Mrs Holland, but wicked as I am,
I read my Bible sometimes, and in it as I read to-day,
I found a verse like this, where friends should 'go
no more out ; ' and there were 'no tears,' and I
wished as I sat down to-night that we were *there* —
not *here* — and that wonderful world had commenced, which makes such promises, and rather than
to write you, I were by your side, and the 'hundred
and forty and four thousand' were chatting pleasantly,
yet not disturbing us.   And I'm half tempted to take
my seat in that Paradise of which the good man
writes, and begin forever and ever *now*, so wondrous
does it seem.   My only sketch, profile, of Heaven is
a large, blue sky, bluer and larger than the *biggest* I
have seen in June, and in it are my friends — all of
them — every one of them — those who are with me
now, and those who were 'parted' as we walked,
and 'snatched up to Heaven.'

If roses had not faded, and frosts had never come,
and one had not fallen here and there whom I could
not waken, there were no need of other Heaven than
the one below — and if God had been here this summer, and seen the things that *I* have seen — I guess
that He would think His Paradise superfluous.   Don't

tell Him, for the world, though, for after all He's said about it, I should like to see what He *was* building for us, with no hammer, and no stone, and no journeyman either.   Dear Mrs Holland, I love, to-night — love you and Dr Holland, and 'time and sense' — and fading things, and things that do *not* fade.

I'm so glad you are not a blossom, for those in my garden fade, and then a 'reaper whose name is Death' has come to get a few to help him make a bouquet for himself, so I'm glad you are not a rose — and I'm glad you are not a bee, for where they go when summer's done, only the thyme knows, and even were you a robin, when the west winds came, you would coolly wink at me, and away, some morning !

As 'little Mrs Holland,' then, I think I love you most, and trust that tiny lady will dwell below while we dwell, and when with many a wonder we seek the new Land, *her* wistful face, *with* ours, shall look the last upon the hills, and first upon — well, *Home !*

Pardon my sanity, Mrs Holland, in a world *in*sane, and love me if you will, for I had rather *be* loved than to be called a king in earth, or a lord in Heaven.

Thank you for your sweet note — the clergy are very well.   Will bring such fragments from them as shall seem me good.   I kiss my paper here for you and Dr Holland — would it were cheeks instead.

Dearly,   Emilie.

P. S. The bobolinks have gone.

[1857 ?]

DEAR SISTER, — After you went, a low wind warbled through the house like a spacious bird, making it high but lonely. When you had gone the love came. I supposed it would. The supper of the heart is when the guest has gone.

Shame is so intrinsic in a strong affection we must all experience Adam's reticence. I suppose the street that the lover travels is thenceforth divine, incapable of turnpike aims.

That you be with me annuls fear and I await Commencement with merry resignation. Smaller than David you clothe me with extreme Goliath.

Friday I tasted life. It was a vast morsel. A circus passed the house — still I feel the red in my mind though the drums are out.

The book you mention, I have not met. Thank you for tenderness.

The lawn is full of south and the odors tangle, and I hear to-day for the first the river in the tree.

You mentioned spring's delaying — I blamed her for the opposite. I would eat evanescence slowly.

Vinnie is deeply afflicted in the death of her dappled cat, though I convince her it is immortal which assists her some. Mother resumes lettuce, involving my transgression — suggestive of yourself, however, which endears disgrace.

'House' is being 'cleaned.' I prefer pestilence. That is more classic and less fell.

Yours was my first arbutus. It was a rosy boast.
I will send you the first witch hazel.

A woman died last week, young and in hope but
a little while — at the end of our garden. I thought
since of the power of Death, not upon affection, but
its mortal signal. It is to us the Nile.

You refer to the unpermitted delight to be with
those we love. I suppose that to be the license not
granted of God.

> Count not that far that can be had,
> Though sunset lie between —
> Nor that adjacent, that beside,
> Is further than the sun.

Love for your embodiment of it.

EMILY.

[1859.]

God bless you, dear Mrs Holland! I read it in
the paper.

I'm so glad it's a little boy, since now the little
sisters have some one to draw them on the sled —
and if a grand old lady you should live to be,
there's something sweet, they say, in a son's arm.

I pray for the tenants of that holy chamber, the
wrestler, and the wrestled for. I pray for distant
father's heart, swollen, happy heart!

Saviour keep them all!

EMILY.

[Autumn, 1859.]

DEAR HOLLANDS, — Belong to me! We have
no fires yet, and the evenings grow cold. To-morrow, stoves are set. How many barefoot shiver I

trust their Father knows who saw not fit to give them shoes.

Vinnie is sick to-night, which gives the world a russet tinge, usually so red. It is only a headache, but when the head aches next to you, it becomes important. When she is well, time leaps. When she is ill, he lags, or stops entirely.

Sisters are brittle things. God was penurious with me, which makes me shrewd with Him.

One is a dainty sum ! One bird, one cage, one flight ; one song in those far woods, as yet suspected by faith only !

This is September, and you were coming in September. Come ! Our parting is too long. There has been frost enough. We must have summer now, and 'whole legions' of daisies.

The gentian is a greedy flower, and overtakes us all. Indeed, this world is short, and I wish, until I tremble, to touch the ones I love before the hills are red — are gray — are white — are 'born again ' ! If we knew how deep the crocus lay, we never should let her go. Still, crocuses stud many mounds whose gardeners till in anguish some tiny, vanished bulb.

We saw you that Saturday afternoon, but heedlessly forgot to ask where you were going, so did not know, and could not write. Vinnie saw Minnie flying by, one afternoon at Palmer. She supposed you were all there on your way from the sea, and untied her fancy ! To say that her fancy wheedled her is superfluous.

We talk of you together, then diverge on life, then hide in you again, as a safe fold. Don't leave us long, dear friends! You know we 're children still, and children fear the dark.

Are you well at home? Do you work now? Has it altered much since I was there? Are the children women, and the women thinking it will soon be afternoon? We will help each other bear our unique burdens.

Is Minnie with you now? Take her our love, if she is. Do her eyes grieve her now? Tell her she may have half ours.

Mother's favorite sister is sick, and mother will have to bid her good-night. It brings mists to us all; — the aunt whom Vinnie visits, with whom she spent, I fear, her last inland Christmas. Does God take care of those at sea? My aunt is such a timid woman!

Will you write to us? I bring you all their loves — *many.*

They tire me.   EMILIE.

[1860.]

How is your little Byron? Hope he gains his foot without losing his genius. Have heard it ably argued that the poet's genius lay in his foot — as the bee's prong and his song are concomitant. Are you stronger than these? To assault so minute a creature seems to me malign, unworthy of Nature — but the frost is no respecter of persons.

I should be glad to be with you, or to open your
letter.   Blossoms belong to the bee, if needs be by
habeas corpus.
EMILY.

Probably about 1861 came this brilliant, yet
half pathetic, arraignment of the friends who
had not written when Emily expected to hear.
Who could resist such a plea?

Friday.

DEAR FRIENDS, — I write to you.   I receive no
letter.

I say 'they dignify my trust.'   I do not disbelieve.
I go again.   *Cardinals* would n't do it.   Cockneys
would n't do it, but I can't *stop* to strut, in a world
where bells toll.   I hear through visitor in town, that
'Mrs Holland is not strong.'   The little peacock in
me, tells me not to inquire again.   Then I remember
my tiny friend — how brief she is — how dear she
is, and the peacock quite dies away.   Now, you need
not speak, for perhaps you are weary, and 'Herod'
requires all your thought, but if you are *well* — let
Annie draw me a little picture of an erect flower;
if you are *ill,* she can hang the flower a little on one
side !

Then, I shall understand, and you need not stop
to write me a letter.   Perhaps you laugh at me !
Perhaps the whole United States are laughing at
me too !   *I* can't stop for that !   *My* business is to
love.   I found a bird, this morning, down — down

— on a little bush at the foot of the garden, and wherefore sing, I said, since nobody *hears?*

One sob in the throat, one flutter of bosom — '*My* business is to *sing*' — and away she rose! How do I know but cherubim, once, themselves, as patient, listened, and applauded her unnoticed hymn?

EMILY.

[1864?]

DEAR SISTER, — Father called to say that our steel-yard was fraudulent, exceeding by an ounce the rates of honest men.   He had been selling oats.   I cannot stop smiling, though it is hours since, that even our steelyard will not tell the truth.

Besides wiping the dishes for Margaret, I wash them now, while she becomes Mrs Lawler, vicarious papa to four previous babes.   Must she not be an adequate bride?

I winced at her loss, because I was in the habit of her, and even a new rolling-pin has an embarrassing element, but to all except anguish, the mind soon adjusts.

It is also November.   The noons are more laconic and the sundowns sterner, and Gibraltar lights make the village foreign.   November always seemed to me the Norway of the year.   —— is still with the sister who put her child in an ice nest last Monday forenoon.   The redoubtable God!   I notice where Death has been introduced, he frequently calls, making it desirable to forestall his advances.

It is hard to be told by the papers that a friend is failing, not even know where the water lies. Incidentally, only, that he comes to land. Is there no voice for these? Where is Love to-day?

Tell the dear Doctor we mention him with a foreign accent, party already to transactions spacious and untold. Nor have we omitted to breathe shorter for our little sister. Sharper than dying is the death for the dying's sake.

News of these would comfort, when convenient or possible.

EMILY.

DEAR SISTER, — It was incredibly sweet that Austin had seen you, and had stood in the dear house which had lost its friend. To see one who had seen you was a strange assurance. It helped dispel the fear that you departed too, for notwithstanding the loved notes and the lovely gift, there lurked a dread that you had gone or would seek to go. 'Where the treasure is,' there is the prospective.

Austin spoke very warmly and strongly of you, and we all felt firmer, and drew a vocal portrait of Kate at Vinnie's request, so vivid that we saw her. . . .

> Not all die early, dying young,
> Maturity of fate
> Is consummated equally
> In ages or a night.
> A hoary boy I 've known to drop
> Whole-statured, by the side
> Of junior of fourscore — 't was act,
> Not period, that died.

EMILY.

Will some one lay this little flower on Mrs
Holland's pillow?

EMILIE.

In handwriting similar to the letters about
1862–68, are several poems, enclosed to the
Hollands, among them, —

> Away from home are some and I,
> An emigrant to be
> In a metropolis of homes
> Is common possibility.
> The habit of a foreign sky
> We, difficult, acquire,
> As children who remain in face,
> The more their feet retire.

And —

> Though my destiny be fustian
> Hers be damask fine —
> Though she wear a silver apron,
> I, a less divine,
>
> Still, my little gypsy being,
> I would far prefer,
> Still my little sunburnt bosom,
> To her rosier.
>
> For when frosts their punctual fingers
> On her forehead lay,
> You and I and Doctor Holland
> Bloom eternally,

Roses of a steadfast summer
In a steadfast land,
Where no autumn lifts her pencil,
And no reapers stand.

In addition to these, many other poems were
sent to the Hollands which have already been
published; all of them, however, showing slight
changes from copies which she retained.

[Autumn, 1876.]

Saturday Eve.

DEAR HOLLANDS, — Good-night! I can't stay
any longer in a world of death. Austin is ill of
fever. I buried my garden last week — our man,
Dick, lost a little girl through the scarlet fever. I
thought perhaps that *you* were dead, and not knowing the sexton's address, interrogate the daisies.
Ah! dainty — dainty Death! Ah! democratic
Death! Grasping the proudest zinnia from my
purple garden, — then deep to his bosom calling
the serf's child!

Say, is he everywhere? Where shall I hide my
things? Who is alive? The woods are dead. Is
Mrs H. alive? Annie and Katie — are they below,
or received to nowhere?

I shall not tell how short time is, for I was told
by lips which sealed as soon as it was said, and the
open revere the shut. You were not here in summer.
Summer? My memory flutters — had I — was there

a summer? You should have seen the fields go
— gay little entomology! Swift little ornithology!
Dancer, and floor, and cadence quite gathered away,
and I, a phantom, to you a phantom, rehearse
the story! An orator of feather unto an audience
of fuzz, — and pantomimic plaudits. 'Quite as good
as a play,' indeed! Tell Mrs Holland she is mine.

Ask her if *vice versa?* Mine is but just the
thief's request — 'Remember me to-day.' Such are
the bright chirographies of the 'Lamb's Book.' Good-
night! My ships are in! — My window overlooks
the wharf! One yacht, and a man-of-war; two
brigs and a schooner! 'Down with the topmast!
Lay her a' hold, a' hold!'   EMILIE.

A letter from Mrs Holland to Emily and her
sister jointly, in 1877, called forth this unique
protest.

SISTER, — A mutual plum is not a plum. I was
too respectful to take the pulp and do not like a
stone.

Send no union letters. The soul must go by
Death alone, so, it must by life, if it is a soul.

If a committee — no matter.

I saw the sunrise on the Alps since I saw you.
Travel why to Nature, when she dwells with us?
Those who lift their hats shall see her, as devout
do God.

I trust you are merry and sound. The chances

are all against the dear, when we are not with them, though paws of principalities cannot affront if we are by.

Dr Vaill called here Monday on his way to your house to get the Doctor to preach for him. Shall search *The Republican* for a brief of the sermon. To-day is very homely and awkward as the homely are who have not mental beauty.

Then follows, —

'The sky is low, the clouds are mean,'

printed at page 103 of the *Poems*, First Series.

[Spring, 1878.]

I thought that 'Birnam Wood' had 'come to Dunsinane.' Where did you pick arbutus? In Broadway, I suppose. They say that God is everywhere, and yet we always think of Him as somewhat of a recluse. . . . It is hard not to hear again that vital 'Sam is coming' — though if grief is a test of a priceless life, he is compensated. He was not ambitious for redemption — that was why it is his. 'To him that hath, shall be given.' Were it not for the eyes, we would know of you oftener. Have they no remorse for their selfishness? 'This tabernacle' is a blissful trial, but the bliss predominates.

I suppose you will play in the water at Alexandria Bay, as the baby does at the tub in the drive. . . . Speak to us when your eyes can spare you, and

'keep us, at home, or by the way,' as the cler-
gyman says, when he folds the church till another
Sabbath.

Lovingly,

EMILY.

[August, 1879.]

LOVED AND LITTLE SISTER, — Vinnie brought in a
sweet pea to-day, which had a pod on the 'off'
side. Startled by the omen, I hasten to you.

An unexpected impediment to my reply to your
dear last, was a call from my Aunt Elizabeth —'the
only male relative on the female side,' and though
many days since, its flavor of court-martial still sets
my spirit tingling.

With what dismay I read of those columns of
kindred in the Bible — the Jacobites and the Jebu-
sites and the Hittites and the Jacqueminots!

I am sure you are better, for no rheumatism in
its senses would stay after the thermometer struck
ninety!

We are revelling in a gorgeous drought.

The grass is painted brown, and how nature would
look in other than the standard colors, we can all
infer. . . . I bade —— call on you, but Vinnie said
you were 'the other side the globe,' yet Vinnie
thinks Vermont is in Asia, so I don't intend to be
disheartened by trifles.

Vinnie has a new pussy that catches a mouse an
hour. We call her the 'minute hand.' . . .

Dr Holland's death, in October of 1881, brought grief to many loving hearts, but to the quiet Amherst household peculiar pain, voiced in the notes to follow.

We read the words but know them not. We are too frightened with sorrow. If that dear, tired one must sleep, could we not see him first?

Heaven is but a little way to one who gave it, here. 'Inasmuch,' to him, how tenderly fulfilled!

Our hearts have flown to you before — our breaking voices follow. How can we wait to take you all in our sheltering arms?

Could there be new tenderness, it would be for you, but the heart is full — another throb would split it — nor would we dare to speak to those whom such a grief removes, but we have somewhere heard 'A little child shall lead them.'

EMILY.

Thursday.

After a while, dear, you will remember that there is a heaven — but you can't now. Jesus will excuse it. He will remember his shorn lamb.

The lost one was on such childlike terms with the Father in Heaven. He has passed from confiding to comprehending — perhaps but a step.

The *safety* of a beloved lost is the first anguish. With you, that is peace.

I shall never forget the Doctor's prayer, my first

morning with you — so simple, so believing. *That*
God must be a friend — *that* was a different God —
and I almost felt warmer myself, in the midst of a
tie so sunshiny.

I am yearning to know if he knew he was fleeing
— if he spoke to you. Dare I ask if he suffered?
Some one will tell me a very little, when they have
the strength. . . . Cling tight to the hearts that will
not let you fall.

EMILY.

Panting to help the dear ones and yet not knowing how, lest any voice bereave them but that loved
voice that will not come, if I can rest them, here is
down — or rescue, here is power.

One who only said 'I am sorry' helped me the
most when father ceased — it was too soon for
language.

Fearing to tell mother, some one disclosed it unknown to us. Weeping bitterly, we tried to console
her. She only replied 'I loved him so.'

Had he a tenderer eulogy?

EMILY.

. . . I know you will live for our sake, dear,
you would not be willing to for your own. That is
the duty which saves. While we are trying for
others, power of life comes back, very faint at first,
like the new bird, but by and by it has wings.

How sweetly you have comforted me — the toil

to comfort you, I hoped never would come. A sorrow on your sunny face is too dark a miracle — but how sweet that he rose in the morning — accompanied by dawn. How lovely that he spoke with you, that memorial time! How gentle that he left the pang he had not time to feel! Bequest of darkness, yet of light, since unborne by him. 'Where thou goest, *we* will go ' — how mutual, how intimate! No solitude receives him, but neighborhood and friend.

Relieved forever of the loss of those that must have fled, but for his sweet haste. Knowing he could not spare *them*, he hurried like a boy from that unhappened sorrow. Death has mislaid his sting — the grave forgot his victory. Because the flake fell not on him, we will accept the drift, and wade where he is lain.

Do you remember the clover leaf? The little hand that plucked it will keep tight hold of mine.

Please give her love to Annie, and Kate, who also gave a father.

EMILY.

[To Mrs Holland, on the marriage of her daughter Annie, December 7, 1881]

SWEET SISTER, — We were much relieved to know that the dear event had occurred without overwhelming any loved one, and perhaps it is sweeter and safer so. I feared much for the parting, to you, to whom parting has come so thickly in the last few days. I knew all would be beautiful, and rejoice it was. Few daughters have the immortality of a father for a bridal gift. Could there be one more costly?

As we never have ceased to think of you, we will more tenderly, now. Confide our happiness to Annie, in her happiness. We hope the unknown balm may ease the balm withdrawn.

You and Katie, the little sisters, lose her, yet obtain her, for each new width of love largens all the rest. Mother and Vinnie think and speak. Vinnie hopes to write. Would that mother could, but her poor hand is idle. Shall I return to you your last and sweetest words — ' But I love you all '?

EMILY.

[Christmas, 1881.]

Dare we wish the brave sister a sweet Christmas, who remembered us punctually in sorrow as in peace?

The broken heart is broadest. Had it come all the way in your little hand, it could not have reached us perfecter, though had it, we should have clutched the hand and forgot the rest.

Fearing the day had associations of anguish to you, I was just writing when your token came. Then, humbled with wonder at your self-forgetting, I delayed till now. Reminded again of gigantic Emily Brontë, of whom her Charlotte said ' Full of ruth for others, on herself she had no mercy.' The hearts that never lean, must fall. To moan is justified.

To thank you for remembering under the piercing circumstances were a profanation.

God bless the hearts that suppose they are beating and are not, and enfold in His infinite tenderness those that do not know they are beating and are.

Shall we wish a triumphant Christmas to the brother withdrawn? Certainly he possesses it.

> How much of Source escapes with thee —
> How chief thy sessions be —
> For thou hast borne a universe
> Entirely away.

With wondering love,

EMILY.

'Whom seeing not, we' clasp.   .

EMILY.

[1883?]

Concerning the little sister, not to assault, not to adjure, but to obtain those constancies which exalt friends, we followed her to St Augustine, since which the trail was lost, or says George Stearns of his alligator, 'there was no such aspect.'

The beautiful blossoms waned at last, the charm of all who knew them, resisting the effort of earth or air to persuade them to root, as the great florist says 'The flower that never will in other climate grow.'

To thank you for its fragrance would be impossible, but then its other blissful traits are more than can be numbered.   And the beloved Christmas, too, for which I never thanked you.   I hope the little heart is well, — *big* would have been the width, — and the health solaced ; any news of her as sweet as the first arbutus.

Emily and Vinnie give the love greater every hour.

CHAPTER V

To Mr Samuel Bowles and Mrs Bowles

A S Emily Dickinson approached middle
life, and even before her thirtieth year,
it seemed to become more and more impossible for her to mingle in general society; and
a growing feeling of shyness, as early as 1862
or 1863, caused her to abstain, sometimes,
from seeing the dearest friends who came to
the house. In spite of her sympathy with
sadness, and her deep apprehension of the
tragic element in life, she was not only keenly
humorous and witty, as already said, but,
while made serious by the insistence of life's
pathos, she was yet at heart as ecstatic as
a bird. This combination of qualities made
her companionship, when she vouchsafed it,
peculiarly breezy and stimulating. Such a
nature must inevitably know more pain than
pleasure.

Passionately devoted to her friends, her happiness in their love and trust was at times
almost too intense to bear; and it will already

have been seen how disproportionately great pain was caused by even comparatively slight separations.   With her, pathos lay very near raillery and badinage, — sadness very near delight.

Whether, in writing her poems, the joy of creating was sufficient, or whether a thought of future and wider recognition ever came, it is certain that during life her friends made her audience. She cared more for appreciation and approval from the few who were dear than for any applause from an impersonal public. She herself writes, ' My friends are my estate.'

All her letters show this rare loyalty of soul, those in the preceding chapter particularly, but none perhaps more strongly than those to Mr and Mrs Bowles. Beginning about 1858, the letters cover a period of twenty-six or twenty-seven years. Often a single short poem comprises the entire letter, — sometimes only four lines, and without title, date, or signature, but unmistakably pertinent to a special occasion or subject.

[Late August, 1858 ?]

AMHERST.

DEAR MR BOWLES, — I got the little pamphlet. I think you sent it to me, though unfamiliar with your hand — I may mistake.

Thank you, if I am right. Thank you, if not,
since here I find bright pretext to ask you how you
are to-night, and for the health of four more,
elder and minor Mary, Sallie and Sam, tenderly to
inquire.

I hope your cups are full.

I hope your vintage is untouched. In such a
porcelain life one likes to be *sure* that all is well
lest one stumble upon one's hopes in a pile of
broken crockery.

My friends are my estate. Forgive me then the
avarice to hoard them! They tell me those were
poor early have different views of gold. I don't
know how that is.

God is not so wary as we, else He would give us
no friends, lest we forget Him! The charms of
the heaven in the bush are superseded, I fear, by
the heaven in the hand, occasionally.

Summer stopped since you were here. Nobody
noticed her — that is, no men and women. Doubtless, the fields are rent by petite anguish, and
'mourners go about' the woods. But this is not
for us. Business enough indeed, our stately resurrection! A special courtesy, I judge, from what the
clergy say! To the 'natural man' bumblebees
would seem an improvement, and a spicing of
birds, but far be it from me to impugn such
majestic tastes!

Our pastor says we are a 'worm.' How is that
reconciled? 'Vain, sinful worm' is possibly of
another species.

Do you think we shall 'see God'? Think of Abraham strolling with Him in genial promenade!

The men are mowing the second hay. The cocks are smaller than the first, and spicier. I would distil a cup, and bear to all my friends, drinking to her no more astir, by beck, or burn, or moor!

Good-night, Mr Bowles. This is what they say who come back in the morning; also the closing paragraph on repealed lips. Confidence in day-break modifies dusk.

Blessings for Mrs Bowles, and kisses for the bairns' lips. We want to see you, Mr Bowles, but spare you the rehearsal of 'familiar truths.'

Good-night,

EMILY.

[Winter, 1858?]

Monday Eve.

DEAR MRS BOWLES, — You send sweet messages. Remembrance is more sweet than robins in May orchards.

I love to trust that round bright fires, some, braver than I, take my pilgrim name. How are papa, mamma, and the little people? . . .

It storms in Amherst five days — it snows, and then it rains, and then soft fogs like veils hang on all the houses, and then the days turn topaz, like a lady's pin.

Thank you for bright bouquet, and afterwards verbena. I made a plant of a little bough of yellow

heliotrope which the bouquet bore me, and call it
Mary Bowles. It is many days since the summer
day when you came with Mr Bowles, and before
another summer day it will be many days. My
garden is a little knoll with faces under it, and only
the pines sing tunes, now the birds are absent. I
cannot walk to the distant friends on nights piercing
as these, so I put both hands on the window-pane,
and try to think how birds fly, and imitate, and fail,
like Mr 'Rasselas.' I could make a balloon of
a dandelion, but the fields are gone, and only ' Professor Lowe ' remains to weep with me. If I built
my house I should like to call you. I talk of all
these things with Carlo, and his eyes grow meaning,
and his shaggy feet keep a slower pace. Are you
safe to-night? I hope you may be glad. I ask
God on my knee to send you much prosperity, few
winter days, and long suns. I have a childish hope
to gather all I love together and sit down beside
and smile. . . .

Will you come to Amherst? The streets are very
cold now, but we will make you warm. But if you
never came, perhaps you could write a letter, saying
how much you would like to, if it were ' God's will.'
I give good-night, and daily love to you and Mr
Bowles.   EMILIE.

[1859.]
                              AMHERST.

I should like to thank dear Mrs Bowles for the
little book, except my cheek is red with shame

because I write so often.   Even the ' lilies of the field ' have their dignities.

Why did you bind it in green and gold ?   The *immortal* colors.   I take it for an emblem.   I never read before what Mr Parker wrote.

I heard that he was ' poison.'   Then I like poison very well.   Austin stayed from service yesterday afternoon, and I . . . found him reading my Christmas gift. . . . I wish the ' faith of the fathers ' did n't wear brogans, and carry blue umbrellas.   I give you all ' New Year ! '   I think you kept gay Christmas, from the friend's account, and can only sigh with one not present at ' John Gilpin,' ' and when he next doth ride a race,' etc.   You picked your berries from my holly.   Grasping Mrs Bowles !

To-day is very cold, yet have I much bouquet upon the window-pane of moss and fern.   I call them saints' flowers, because they do not romp as other flowers do, but stand so still and white.

The snow is very tall, . . . which makes the trees so low that they tumble my hair, when I cross the bridge.

I think there will be no spring this year, the flowers are gone so far.   Let us have spring in our heart, and never mind the orchises ! . . . Please have my love, mother's, and Vinnie's.   Carlo sends a brown kiss, and pussy a gray and white one, to each of the children.

Please, now I write so often, make lamplighter of me, then I shall not have lived in vain.

Dear Mrs Bowles, dear Mr Bowles, dear Sally —
Sam and Mamie, now all shut your eyes, while I do
benediction !

Lovingly,   EMILY.

[Written in 1861, on the birth of a son.]

DEAR MARY, — Can you leave your flower long
enough just to look at mine?

Which is the prettiest? I shall tell you myself,
some day. I used to come to comfort you, but now
to tell you how glad I am, and how glad we all are.
. . . You must not stay in New York any more —
you must come back now, and bring the blanket to
Massachusetts where we can all look. What a
responsible shepherd ! Four lambs in one flock !
Shall you be glad to see us, or shall we seem old-
fashioned, by the face in the crib?

Tell him I 've got a pussy for him, with a spotted
gown ; and a dog with ringlets.

We have very cold days since you went away, and
I think you hear the wind blow far as the Brevoort
House, it comes from so far, and crawls so. Don't
let it blow baby away. Will you call him Robert
for me? He is the bravest man alive, but *his* boy
has no mamma. That makes us all weep, don't it?

Good-night, Mary.

EMILY.

One of the very few of Emily Dickinson's
verses named by herself was sent Mrs Bowles
soon after the preceding letter.

BABY.

Teach him, when he makes the names,
Such an one to say
On his babbling, berry lips
As should sound to me —
Were my ear as near his nest
As my thought, to-day —
As should sound — ' forbid us not ' —
Some like ' Emily.'

[August, 1861.]

MARY, — I do not know of you, a long while.
I remember you — several times.   I wish I knew if
you kept me?   The doubt, like the mosquito,
buzzes round my faith.   We are all human, Mary,
until we are divine, and to some of us, that is far
off, and to some as near as the lady ringing at the
door; perhaps *that's* what alarms.   I say I will go
myself — I cross the river, and climb the fence —
now I am at the gate, Mary — now I am in the hall
— now I am looking your heart in the eye !

Did it wait for me — did it go with the company?
Cruel company, who have the stocks, and farms,
and creeds — and *it* has just its heart !   I hope you
are glad, Mary; no pebble in the brook to-day — no
film on noon.

I can think how you look; you can't think how I
look; I 've got more freckles, since you saw me,

playing with the school-boys; then I pare the
'Juneating' to make the pie, and get my fingers
'tanned.'

Summer went very fast — she got as far as the
woman from the hill, who brings the blueberry, and
that is a long way. I shall have no winter this
year, on account of the soldiers. Since I cannot
weave blankets or boots, I thought it best to
omit the season. Shall present a 'memorial' to
God when the maples turn. Can I rely on your
'name'?

How is your garden, Mary? Are the pinks true,
and the sweet williams faithful? I 've got a geranium like a sultana, and when the humming-
birds come down, geranium and I shut our eyes,
and go far away.

Ask 'Mamie' if I shall catch her a butterfly with
a vest like a Turk? I will, if she will build him a
house in her 'morning-glory.'

Vinnie would send her love, but she put on a
white frock, and went to meet to-morrow — a few
minutes ago; mother would send her love, but she
is in the 'eave spout,' sweeping up a leaf that blew
in last November; I brought my own, myself, to
you and Mr Bowles.

Please remember me, because I remember you —
always.

Then follows the poem beginning ' My river
runs to thee,' published in the First Series of
the *Poems*, page 54.

Don't cry, dear Mary. Let us do that for you, because you are too tired now. We don't know how dark it is, but if you are at sea, perhaps when we say that we are there, you won't be as afraid.

The waves are very big, but every one that covers you, covers us, too.

Dear Mary, you can't see us, but we are close at your side. May we comfort you?

Lovingly,

EMILY.

[Autumn, 1861.]

FRIEND, SIR, — I did not see you. I am very sorry. Shall I keep the wine till you come again, or send it in by Dick? It is now behind the door in the library, also an unclaimed flower. I did not know you were going so soon. Oh! my tardy feet.

Will you not come again?

Friends are gems, infrequent. Potosi is a care, sir. I guard it reverently, for I could not afford to be poor now, after affluence. I hope the hearts in Springfield are not so heavy as they were. God bless the hearts in Springfield.

I am happy you have a horse. I hope you will get stalwart, and come and see us many years.

I have but two acquaintance, the 'quick and the dead' — and would like more.

I write you frequently, and am much ashamed. My voice is not quite loud enough to cross so many fields, which will, if you please, apologize for my pencil.

Will you take my love to Mrs Bowles, whom I remember every day?

EMILIE.

Vinnie hallos from the world of night-caps, 'don't forget her love.'

[January, 1862.]

DEAR FRIEND, — Are you willing? I am so far from land. To offer you the cup, it might some Sabbath come *my* turn. Of wine how solemn-full!

Did you get the doubloons — did you vote upon 'Robert'? You said you would come in February. Only three weeks more to wait at the gate!

While you are sick, we — are homesick. Do you look out to-night? The moon rides like a girl through a topaz town. I don't think we shall ever be merry again — you are ill so long. When did the dark happen?

I skipped a page to-night, because I come so often, now, I might have tired you.

That page is fullest, though.

Vinnie sends her love. I think father and mother care a great deal for you, and hope you may be well. When you tire with pain, to know that eyes would cloud, in Amherst — might that comfort, *some ?*

EMILY.

We never forget Mary.

DEAR MR BOWLES, — Thank you.

> Faith is a fine invention
> When gentlemen can see!
> But microscopes are prudent
> In an emergency![1]

You spoke of the 'East.'   I have thought about it this winter.

Don't you think you and I should be shrewder to take the mountain road?

That bareheaded life, under the grass, worries one like a wasp.

The rose is for Mary.

EMILY.

> The zeros taught us phosphorus —
> We learned to like the fire
> By playing glaciers when a boy,
> And tinder guessed by power
>
> Of opposite to balance odd,
> If white, a red must be![2]
> Paralysis, our primer dumb
> Unto vitality.

I could n't let Austin's note go, without a word.

EMILY.

[1] Second Series, page 53.

[2] The poems enclosed in letters to friends are often slightly different from her own copies preserved in the manuscript volumes. This line, for instance, in another place reads 'Eclipses suns imply.'

Sunday Night.

DEAR MARY, — Could you leave ‘Charlie’ long enough? Have you time for *me*? I sent Mr Bowles a little note, last Saturday morning, asking him to do an errand for me.

I forgot he was going to Washington, or I should n't have troubled him, so late. Now, Mary, I fear he did not get it, and *you* tried to do the errand for me — and it troubled you. Did it? Will you tell me? Just say with your pencil ‘It did n't tire me, Emily,’ and then I shall be sure, for with all your care, I would not have taxed you for the world.

You never refused me, Mary, you cherished me many times, but I thought it must seem so selfish to ask the favor of Mr Bowles just as he went from home, only I forgot that. Tell me to-night just a word, Mary, with your own hand, so I shall know I harassed none — and I will be *so* glad.

Austin told us of Charlie — I send a rose for his small hands.

Put it in, when he goes to sleep, and then he will dream of Emily, and when you bring him to Amherst we shall be ‘old friends.’ Don't love him so well, you know, as to forget us. We shall wish he was n't *there*, if you do, I 'm afraid, sha'n't we?

I 'll remember you, if you like me to, while Mr Bowles is gone, and that will stop the lonely, some, but I cannot agree to stop when he gets home from Washington.

Good-night, Mary. You won't forget my little note, to-morrow, in the mail. It will be the first one you ever wrote me in your life, and yet, was I the little friend a long time? *Was* I, Mary?

EMILY.

[March, 1862.]

Perhaps you thought I did n't care — because I stayed out, yesterday. I *did* care, Mr Bowles. I pray for your sweet health to Allah every morning, but something troubled me, and I knew you needed light and air, so I did n't come. Nor have I the conceit that you *noticed* me — but I could n't bear that you, or Mary, so gentle to me, should think me forgetful.

It 's little at the most, we can do for ours, and we must do *that* flying, or our things are flown!

Dear friend, I wish you were well.

It grieves me till I cannot speak, that you are suffering. Won't you come back? Can't I bring you something? My little balm might be o'erlooked by wiser eyes, you know. Have you tried the breeze that swings the sign, or the hoof of the dandelion? *I* own 'em — wait for mine! This is all I have to say. Kinsmen need say nothing, but ' Swiveller ' may be sure of the

' MARCHIONESS.'

Love for Mary.

DEAR FRIEND, — . . . Austin is disappointed — he expected to see you to-day. He is sure you won't go to sea without first speaking to him. I presume if Emily and Vinnie knew of his writing, they would entreat him to ask you not.

Austin is chilled by Frazer's murder.[1] He says his brain keeps saying over ' Frazer is killed ' — ' Frazer is killed,' just as father told it to him. Two or three words of lead, that dropped so deep they keep weighing. Tell Austin how to get over them !

He is very sorry you are not better. He cares for you when at the office, and afterwards, too, at home ; and sometimes wakes at night, with a worry for you he did n't finish quite by day. He would not like it that I betrayed him, so you 'll never tell. . . .

Mary sent beautiful flowers. Did she tell you ?

[Spring, 1862.]

DEAR FRIEND, — The hearts in Amherst ache to-night — you could not know how hard. They thought they could not wait, last night, until the engine sang a pleasant tune that time, because that you were coming. The flowers waited, in the vase, and love got peevish, watching. A railroad person rang, to bring an evening paper — Vinnie tipped pussy over, in haste to let you in, and I, for joy and dignity, held tight in my chair. My hope put out a petal.

You would come, to-day, — but . . . we don't be-

---

[1] A son of President Stearns of Amherst College, who was killed during the war, 13th March, 1862.

lieve it, now; ' Mr Bowles not coming ! '   Would n't
you, to-morrow, and this but be a bad dream, gone
by next morning?

Please do not take our *spring* away, since you blot
summer out !   We cannot count our tears for this,
because they drop so fast. . . .

Dear friend, we meant to make *you* brave, but
moaned before we thought. . . . If you 'll be sure
and get well, we 'll try to bear it.   If we could only
care the less, it would be so much easier.   Your
letter troubled my throat.   It gave that little scald-
ing we could not know the reason for till we grew
far up.

I must do my good-night in crayon I meant to in
red.

Love for Mary.

EMILY.

After Mr Bowles had sailed for Europe,
Emily sent this quaintly consoling note to
Springfield.

[Early Summer, 1862.]

DEAR MARY, — When the best is gone, I know
that other things are not of consequence.   The
heart wants what it wants, or else it does not
care.

You wonder why I write so.   Because I cannot
help.   I like to have you know some care — so
when your life gets faint for its other life, you can
lean on us.   We won't break, Mary.   We look very
small, but the reed can carry weight.

Not to see what we love is very terrible, and talking does n't ease it, and nothing does but just itself. The eyes and hair we chose are all there are — to us. Is n't it so, Mary?

I often wonder how the love of Christ is done when that below holds so.

I hope the little 'Robert' coos away the pain. Perhaps your flowers help, some. . . .

The frogs sing sweet to-day — they have such pretty, lazy times — how nice to be a frog! . . .

Mother sends her love to you — she has a sprained foot, and can go but little in the house, and not abroad at all.

Don't dishearten, Mary, we 'll keep thinking of you. Kisses for all.

EMILY.

[To Mr Bowles, June, 1862.]

DEAR FRIEND, — You go away — and where you go we cannot come — but then the months have names — and each one comes but once a year — and though it seems they never could, they sometimes do, go by.

We hope you are more well than when you lived in America, and that those foreign people are kind, and true, to you. We hope you recollect each life you left behind, even ours, the least.

We wish we knew how Amherst looked, in your memory. Smaller than it did, maybe, and yet things swell, by leaving, if big in themselves.

We hope you will not alter, but be the same we grieved for when the *China* sailed.

If you should like to hear the news, we did not die here — we did not change.   We have the guests we did, except yourself — and the roses hang on the same stems as before you went.   Vinnie trains the honeysuckle, and the robins steal the string for nests — quite, quite as they used to.

I have the errand from my heart — I might forget to tell it.   Would you please to come home?   The long life's years are scant, and fly away, the Bible says, like a told story — and sparing is a solemn thing, somehow, it seems to me — and I grope fast, with my fingers, for all out of my sight I own, to get it nearer.

I had one letter from Mary.   I think she tries to be patient — but you would n't want her to succeed, would you, Mr Bowles?

It 's fragrant news, to know they pine, when we are out of sight.

It is 'most Commencement.   The little cousin from Boston has come, and the hearts in Pelham have an added thrill.   We shall miss you, most, dear friend, who annually smiled with us, at the gravities.   I question if even Dr Vaill have his wonted applause.

Should anybody, where you go, talk of Mrs Browning, you must hear for us, and if you touch her grave, put one hand on the head, for me — her unmentioned mourner.

Father and mother, and Vinnie and Carlo, send their love to you, and warm wish for your health — and I am taking lessons in prayer, so to coax God to keep you safe. Good-night, dear friend. You sleep so far, how can I know you hear?

EMILY.

DEAR FRIEND, — I cannot see you. You will not less believe me. That you return to us alive is better than a summer, and more to hear your voice below than news of any bird.

EMILY.

[August, 1862.]

DEAR MR BOWLES, — Vinnie is trading with a tin peddler — buying water-pots for me to sprinkle geraniums with when you get home next winter, and she has gone to the war.

Summer is n't so long as it was, when we stood looking at it before you went away; and when I finish August, we 'll hop the autumn very soon, and then 't will be yourself.

I don't know how many will be glad to see you, — because I never saw your whole friends, but I have heard that in large cities noted persons chose you — though how glad those I know will be, is easier told.

I tell you, Mr Bowles, it is a suffering to have a sea — no care how blue — between your soul and you.

The hills you used to love when you were in Northampton, miss their old lover, could they speak; and the puzzled look deepens in Carlo's forehead as the days go by and you never come.

I 've learned to read the steamer place in newspapers now.   It 's 'most like shaking hands with you, or more like your ringing at the door.

We reckon your coming by the fruit.   When the grape gets by, and the pippin and the chestnut — when the days are a little short by the clock, and a little long by the want — when the sky has new red gowns, and a purple bonnet — then we say you will come.   I am glad that kind of time goes by.

It is easier to look behind at a pain, than to see it coming.

A soldier called, a morning ago, and asked for a nosegay to take to battle.   I suppose he thought we kept an aquarium.

How sweet it must be to one to come home, whose home is in so many houses, and every heart a ' best room.'   I mean you, Mr Bowles. . . . Have not the clovers names to the bees?

EMILY.

> Before he comes
> We weigh the time,
> 'T is heavy, and 't is light.
> When he departs
> An emptiness
> Is the superior freight.

EMILY.

While asters
On the hill
Their everlasting fashions set,
And covenant gentians frill !

EMILY.

[Late Autumn, 1862.]

So glad we are, a stranger 'd deem
'T was sorry that we were ;
For where the holiday should be
There publishes a tear ;
Nor how ourselves be justified,
Since grief and joy are done
So similar, an optizan
Could not decide between.

[Early Winter, 1862.]

DEAR FRIEND, — Had we the art like you, to endow so many, by just recovering our health, 't would give us tender pride, nor could we keep the news, but carry it to you, who seem to us to own it most.

So few that live have life, it seems of quick importance not one of those escape by death. And since you gave us fear, congratulate us for ourselves — you give us safer peace.

How extraordinary that life's large population contain so few of power to us — and those a vivid species who leave no mode, like Tyrian dye.

Remembering these minorities, permit our gratitude for you. We ask that you be cautious, for many sakes, excelling ours. To recapitulate the stars were useless as supreme. Yourself is yours, dear friend, but ceded, is it not, to here and there a minor life? Do not defraud these, for gold may be bought, and purple may be bought, but the sale of the spirit never did occur.

Do not yet work. No public so exorbitant of any as its friend, and we can wait your health. Besides, there is an idleness more tonic than toil.

> The loss of sickness — was it loss?
> Or that ethereal gain
> You earned by measuring the grave,
> Then measuring the sun.

Be sure, dear friend, for want you have estates of lives.

EMILY.

[With Flowers.]

> If she had been the mistletoe,
> And I had been the rose,
> How gay upon your table
> My velvet life to close!
> Since I am of the Druid,
> And she is of the dew,
> I 'll deck tradition's buttonhole,
> And send the rose to you.

E.

DEAR MR BOWLES, — I can't thank you any more. You are thoughtful so many times you

grieve me always; *now* the old words are numb,
and there are n't any new ones.

Brooks are useless in freshet time. When you
come to Amherst — please God it were to-day — I
will tell you about the picture — if I *can*, I will.

> *Speech* is a prank of Parliament,
> *Tears* a trick of the nerve, —
> But the heart with the heaviest freight on
> Does n't always swerve.
>
> EMILY.

Perhaps you think me stooping!
I 'm not ashamed of that!
Christ stooped until he touched the grave!
Do those at sacrament
Commemorate dishonor —
Or love, annealed of love,
Until it bend as low as death
Re-royalized above?

> The juggler's hat her country is,
> The mountain gorse the bee 's.

> I stole them from a bee,
> Because — thee!
> Sweet plea —
> He pardoned me!
>
> EMILY.

Besides the verses given here, many others
were sent to Mr and Mrs Bowles, as to the
Hollands, which, having already been published

in one or the other volume of the *Poems*, will not be reprinted.

[Summer, 1863.]

DEAR FRIENDS, — I am sorry you came, because you went away.

Hereafter, I will pick no rose, lest it fade or prick me.

I would like to have you dwell here.

Though it is almost nine o'clock, the skies are gay and yellow, and there's a purple craft or so, in which a friend could sail. To-night looks like 'Jerusalem'! . . . I hope we may all behave so as to reach Jerusalem.

How are your hearts to-day? Ours are pretty well. I hope your tour was bright, and gladdened Mrs Bowles. Perhaps the retrospect will call you back some morning.

You shall find us all at the gate if you come in a hundred years, just as we stood that day. If it become of 'jasper' previously, you will not object, so that we lean there still, looking after you.

I rode with Austin this morning. He showed me mountains that touched the sky, and brooks that sang like bobolinks. Was he not very kind? I will give them to you, for they are mine, and 'all things are mine,' excepting 'Cephas and Apollos,' for whom I have no taste. Vinnie's love brims mine.

Take

EMILIE.

DEAR MRS BOWLES, — Since I have no sweet flower to send you, I enclose my heart. A little one, sunburnt, half broken sometimes, yet close as the spaniel to its friends. Your flowers come from heaven, to which, if I should ever go, I will pluck you palms.

My words are far away when I attempt to thank you, so take the silver tear instead, from my full eye.

You have often remembered me.

I have little dominion. Are there not wiser than I, who, with curious treasure, could requite your gift?

Angels fill the hand that loaded

EMILY'S.

Nature and God, I neither knew,
Yet both, so well knew me
They startled, like executors
Of an identity.
Yet neither told, that I could learn;
My secret as secure
As Herschel's private interest,
Or Mercury's affair.

[1863.]

DEAR FRIEND, — You remember the little ' meeting ' we held for you last spring? We met again, Saturday.

'T was May when we ' adjourned,' but then adjourns are all. The meetings were alike, Mr Bowles.

The topic did not tire us, so we chose no new.
We, voted to remember you, so long as both should
live, including immortality ; to count you, as ourselves, except sometimes more tenderly, as now,
when you are ill, and we, the haler of the two —
and so I bring the bond we sign so many times, for
you to read when chaos comes, or treason, or decay,
still witnessing for morning. . . . We hope our joy
to see you gave of its own degree to you. We pray
for your new health, the prayer that goes not down
when they shut the church. We offer you our cups
— stintless, as to the bee, — the lily, her new
liquors.

Would you like summer?   Taste of ours.

Spices? Buy here !

Ill !   We have berries, for the parching !

Weary !   Furloughs of down !

Perplexed !   Estates of violet trouble ne'er
looked on !

Captive !   We bring reprieve of roses !

Fainting !   Flasks of air !

Even for Death, a fairy medicine.

But, which is it, sir?   EMILY.

<blockquote>

I 'll send the feather from my hat !
Who knows but at the sight of *that*
My sovereign will relent?
As trinket, worn by faded child,
Confronting eyes long comforted
Blisters the adamant !

</blockquote>

EMILY.

Her breast is fit for pearls,
But I was not a diver.
Her brow is fit for thrones,
But I had not a crest.
Her heart is fit for rest —
I, a sparrow, build there
Sweet of twigs and twine,
My perennial nest.

[1864?]

DEAR FRIEND, — How hard to thank you — but the large heart requites itself. Please to need me. I wanted to ask you to receive Mr Browning from me, but you denied my Brontë — so I did not dare.

Is it too late now? I should like so much to remind you how kind you had been to me.

You could choose — as you did before — if it would not be obnoxious — except where you 'measured by your heart,' you should measure this time by mine. I wonder which would be biggest !

Austin told, Saturday morning, that you were not so well. 'T was sundown, all day, Saturday — and Sunday such a long bridge no news of you could cross !

Teach us to miss you less because the fear to miss you more haunts us all the time. We did n't care so much, once. I wish it was then, now, but you kept tightening, so it can't be stirred to-day. You did n't mean to be worse, did you? Was n't it a mistake?

Won't you decide soon to be the strong man we first knew? 'T would lighten things so much — and yet that man was not so dear — I guess you'd better not.

We pray for you, every night. A homely shrine our knee, but Madonna looks at the heart first.

Dear friend — don't discourage !

Affectionately,

EMILY.

No wilderness can be
Where *this* attendeth thee —
No desert noon,
No fear of frost to come
Haunt the perennial bloom,
But certain June !

EMILY.

The following lines, sent with flowers, have almost as quaint and 'seventeenth century' a flavor as the now famous quatrain beginning, —

'A death-blow is a life-blow to some.'

If recollecting were forgetting
Then I remember not.
And if forgetting, recollecting,
How near I had forgot !
And if to miss were merry,
And if to mourn were gay,
How very blithe the fingers
That gathered this, to-day !

EMILIE.

Other verses, sent at different times, were
written in the same general hand, — that of
the early middle period, from about 1863 to
1870; among them : —

> ' They have not chosen me,' he said,
> ' But I have chosen them.'
> Brave, broken-hearted statement
> Uttered in Bethlehem !

> *I* could not have told it,
> But since Jesus dared,
> Sovereign ! know a daisy
> Thy dishonor shared.   EMILY.

Saturday.

Mother never asked a favor of Mr Bowles before
— that he accept from her the little barrel of apples.
' Sweet apples,' she exhorts me, with an occasional
Baldwin for Mary and the squirrels.

                                              EMILY.

> Just once — oh ! least request !
> Could adamant refuse
> So small a grace,
> So scanty put,
> Such agonizing terms ?

> Would not a God of flint
> Be conscious of a sigh,
> As down his heaven dropt remote,
> ' Just once, sweet Deity ? '

Saturday

Mother never asked
a favor of Mr Bowles
before — that he
accept from her
the little Barrel
of Apples.
"Sweet Apples" — She
exhorts me — with an
occasional Baldwin —
for Mary, and the
Squirrels   Emily

A spray of white pine was enclosed with this
note : —

> A feather from the whippoorwill
> That everlasting sings !
> Whose galleries are sunrise,
> Whose opera the springs,
> Whose emerald nest the ages spin
> Of mellow, murmuring thread,
> Whose beryl egg, what school boys-hunt
> In ' recess ' overhead !
>
> EMILY.

We part with the river at the flood through a
timid custom, though with the same waters we have
often played.

EMILY.

[1865 ?]

DEAR FRIEND, — Vinnie accidentally mentions
that you hesitated between the *Theophilus* and
the *Junius*.

Would you confer so sweet a favor as to accept
that too, when you come again?

I went to the room as soon as you left, to confirm
your presence, recalling the Psalmist's sonnet to
God beginning

> I have no life but this —
> To lead it here,
> Nor any death but lest
> Dispelled from there.
> Nor tie to earths to come,
> Nor action new,
> Except through this extent —
> The love of you.

It is strange that the most intangible thing is the most adhesive.

Your ' rascal.'

I washed the adjective.

[1868 ?]

I should think you would have few letters, for your own are so noble that they make men afraid. And sweet as your approbation is, it is had in fear, — lest your depth convict us.

You compel us each to remember that when water ceases to rise, it has commenced falling. That is the law of flood.

The last day that I saw you was the newest and oldest of my life.

Resurrection can come but once, first, to the same house.   Thank you for leading us by it.

Come always, dear friend, but refrain from going. You spoke of not liking to be forgotten.   Could you, though you would?

Treason never knew you.

EMILY.

[1869 ?]

DEAR FRIEND, — You have the most triumphant face out of Paradise, probably because you are there constantly, instead of ultimately.

Ourselves we do inter with sweet derision the channel of the dust; who once achieves, invalidates the balm of that religion, that doubts as fervently as it believes.

EMILY.

Wednesday.

Dear Mr Bowles's note, of itself a blossom, came only to-night.

I am glad it lingered, for each was all the heart could hold.

EMILY.

Of your exquisite act there can be no acknowledgment but the ignominy that grace gives.

EMILY.

Could mortal lip divine
The undeveloped freight
Of a delivered syllable,
'T would crumble with the weight !

[1873.]

DEAR FRIEND, — It was so delicious to see you — a peach before the time — it makes all seasons possible, and zones a caprice.

We, who arraign the *Arabian Nights* for their understatement, escape the stale sagacity of supposing them sham.

We miss your vivid face, and the besetting accents you bring from your Numidian haunts.

Your coming welds anew that strange trinket of life which each of us wear and none of us own; and the phosphorescence of yours startles us for its permanence.

Please rest the life so many own — for gems abscond.

In your own beautiful words — for the voice is the palace of all of us, —

'Near, but remote.'

EMILY.

[1874.]

DEAR FRIEND, — The paper wanders so I cannot write my name on it, so I give you father's portrait instead.

> As summer into autumn slips
> And yet we sooner say
> 'The summer' than 'the autumn,' lest
> We turn the sun away,
>
> And almost count it an affront
> The presence to concede
> Of one however lovely, not
> The one that we have loved, —
>
> So we evade the charge of years,
> One, one attempting shy
> The circumvention of the shaft
> Of life's declivity.   EMILY.

If we die, will you come for us, as you do for father?

'Not born,' yourself 'to die,' you must reverse us all.

> Last to adhere
> When summers swerve away —
> Elegy of
> Integrity.

To remember our own Mr Bowles is all we can do.
With grief it is done, so warmly and long, it can
never be new.

EMILY.

In January of 1878, Mr Bowles died, leaving
a sense of irreparable loss, not only to his
friends, but to his great constituency through
The Republican, into whose success he had
woven the very tissue of his own magnetic
personality.

[January, 1878.]

I hasten to you, Mary, because no moment must
be lost when a heart is breaking, for though it broke
so long, each time is newer than the last, if it broke
truly.   To be willing that I should speak to you was
so generous, dear.

Sorrow almost resents love, it is so inflamed.

I am glad if the broken words helped you.   I
had not hoped so much, I felt so faint in uttering
them, thinking of your great pain.   Love makes us
' heavenly ' without our trying in the least.   'T is
easier than a Saviour — it does not stay on high and
call us to its distance ; its low ' Come unto me '
begins in every place.   It makes but one mistake,
it tells us it is ' rest ' — perhaps its toil is rest, but
what we have not known we shall know again, that
divine ' again ' for which we are all breathless.

I am glad you ' work.'   Work is a bleak redeemer, but it does redeem; it tires the flesh so that can't tease the spirit.

Dear 'Mr Sam' is very near, these midwinter days. When purples come on Pelham, in the afternoon, we say 'Mr Bowles's colors.' I spoke to him once of his Gem chapter, and the beautiful eyes rose till they were out of reach of mine, in some hallowed fathom.

Not that he goes — we love him more who led us while he stayed. Beyond earth's trafficking frontier, for what he moved, he made.

Mother is timid and feeble, but we keep her with us. She thanks you for remembering her, and never forgets you. . . . Your sweet 'and left me all alone,' consecrates your lips.

EMILY.

[Spring, 1878.]

Had you never spoken to any, dear, they would not upbraid you, but think of you more softly, as one who had suffered too much to speak. To forget you would be impossible, had we never seen you; for you were his for whom we moan while consciousness remains. As he was himself Eden, he is with Eden, for we cannot become what we were not.

I felt it sweet that you needed me — though but a simple shelter I will always last. I hope your boys and girls assist his dreadful absence, for sorrow does not stand so still on their flying hearts.

How fondly we hope they look like him — that his beautiful face may be abroad.

Was not his countenance on earth graphic as a spirit's? The time will be long till you see him, dear, but it will be short, for have we not each our heart to dress — heavenly as his?

He is without doubt with my father. Thank you for thinking of him, and the sweet, last respect you so faithfully paid him.

Mother is growing better, though she cannot stand, and has not power to raise her head for a glass of water. She thanks you for being sorry, and speaks of you with love. . . . Your timid 'for his sake,' recalls that sheltering passage, 'for his sake who loved us, and gave himself to die for us.'

EMILY.

[1879.]

How lovely to remember! How tenderly they told of you! Sweet toil for smitten hands to console the smitten!

Labors as endeared may engross our lost. Buds of other days quivered in remembrance. Hearts of other days lent their solemn charm.

Life of flowers lain in flowers — what a home of dew! And the bough of ivy; was it as you said? Shall I plant it softly?

There were little feet, white as alabaster.

Dare I chill them with the soil?

Nature is our eldest mother, she will do no harm.

Let the phantom love that enrolls the sparrow shield you softer than a child.

[April, 1880.]

DEAR MARY, — The last April that father lived, lived I mean below, there were several snow-storms, and the birds were so frightened and cold, they sat by the kitchen door. Father went to the barn in his slippers and came back with a breakfast of grain for each, and hid himself while he scattered it, lest it embarrass them. Ignorant of the name or fate of their benefactor, their descendants are singing this afternoon.

As I glanced at your lovely gift, his April returned. I am powerless toward your tenderness.

Thanks of other days seem abject and dim, yet antiquest altars are the fragrantest. The past has been very near this week, but not so near as the future — both of them pleading, the latter priceless.

David's grieved decision haunted me when a little girl. I hope he has found Absalom.

Immortality as a guest is sacred, but when it becomes as with you and with us, a member of the family, the tie is more vivid. . . .

If affection can reinforce, you, dear, shall not fall.

EMILY.

[Probably the famous 'Yellow Day,' September 6, 1881.]
Tuesday.

DEAR MARY, — I give you only a word this mysterious morning in which we must light the lamps to see each other's faces, thanking you for the trust. too confiding for speech.

You spoke of enclosing the face of your child. As it was not there, forgive me if I tell you, lest even the copy of sweetness abscond; and may I trust you received the flower the mail promised to take you, my foot being incompetent?

The timid mistake about being 'forgotten,' shall I caress or reprove? Mr Samuel's 'sparrow' does not 'fall' without the fervent 'notice.'

'Would you see us, would Vinnie?' Oh, my doubting Mary! Were you and your brave son in my father's house, it would require more prowess than mine to resist seeing you.

Shall I still hope for the picture? And please address to my full name, as the little note was detained and opened, the name being so frequent in town, though not an Emily but myself.

Vinnie says 'give her my love, and tell her I would delight to see her;' and mother combines.

There should be no tear on your cheek, dear, had my hand the access to brush it away.

EMILY.

[1881.]

' DEAR MARY, — To have been the mother of the beautiful face, is of itself fame, and the look of

Arabia in the eyes is like Mr Samuel. 'Mr Samuel' is his memorial name. 'Speak, that we may see thee,' and Gabriel no more ideal than his swift eclipse. Thank you for the beauty, which I reluctantly return, and feel like committing a 'startling fraud' in that sweet direction. If her heart is as magical as her face, she will wreck many a spirit, but the sea is ordained.

Austin looked at her long and earnestly.

'Yes, it is Sam's child.' His Cashmere confederate. It is best, dear, you have so much to do. Action is redemption.

'And again a little while and ye shall not see me,' Jesus confesses is temporary.

Thank you indeed.

EMILY.

END OF VOL. I.

V ٢ : ٧"
ﺑﺎﺱ

Lightning Source UK Ltd.
Milton Keynes UK
UKHW022110080223
416681UK00011B/2711